This planner belongs to...
(fill in your family's details below)

TO A
WONDERF...
MY GOAL IS TO HELP INSPIRE
YOU IN THE KITCHEN AND TAKE
THE STRESS OUT OF FEEDING
YOUR FAMILY. I HOPE THIS
PLANNER HELPS DO THAT!
LOVE REBECCA & NINA XX

Name...

Age..

Favourite food / meal ....

....

Still learning to love: food / meal...................

....

Name...

Age..

Favourite food / meal ....

....

Still learning to love: food / meal...................

....

Name...

Age..

Favourite food / meal ....

....

Still learning to love: food / meal...................

....

Name...

Age..

Favourite food / meal ....

....

Still learning to love: food / meal...................

....

Name...

Age..

Favourite food / meal ....

....

Still learning to love: food / meal...................

....

Contents

Sunshine
Peach Muffins,
page 72

WELCOME TO YOUR FAMILY MEAL PLANNER

Here, you will find space to feel inspired to cook healthy, quick and easy meals for your family. With just a little planning, you can cut down on food waste and save yourself time, money and, most importantly, your sanity! I've included some advice on weaning – so that you can start using this planner as soon as you start to introduce your baby to solid foods – as well as my top tips for meal planning, efficient shopping and store-cupboard staples. Let's get started.

GF Gluten-free	**V** Vegetarian	**DF** Dairy-free
EF Egg-free	**Vg** Vegan	

Whenever you see an * next to the letters in the symbol, this indicates that the recipe can be adapted to suit this dietary requirement. Please take care and look for the substitutions listed in the ingredients.

THE BENEFITS OF EATING TOGETHER

Feeding your loved ones one meal and enjoying it together as a family has so many benefits, for example:

- You will show baby how to eat through modelling, which teaches them the physical motions of picking up food, bringing it to their mouths and processing it efficiently, whether that's chomping on a piece of corn on the cob or dipping fritters into yogurt. Consistent exposure to family eating environments will encourage development of dexterity, cutlery skills and drinking through an open cup.

- Combats fussy eating – cooking a varied diet to eat together helps little ones to reduce their food fussiness, by learning from your eating actions as well as exposing them to a wide variety of flavours and textures.

- It takes the stress away – forget cooking three times per meal because baby needs one thing, older siblings another, and the adults want something else.

- It encourages a good routine for your family. By sticking to a similar environment at every mealtime (preferably around a table), your child will be able to differentiate between playtime and eating time.

- Eating together encourages us adults to slow down and give our undivided attention to our little one while they're eating. It's easy to get distracted by the pile of washing to fold, but eating together forces us to sit down and make the eating environment enjoyable for our children. Making mealtimes fun will ensure that our kiddos grow to have a positive attitude towards food.

WHAT FOODS TO AVOID SERVING TO YOUR LITTLE ONES

To safely eat the same meal together, there are a few things to bear in mind. Firstly, ensure that the food you are cooking is suitable for your child's age. Here are a few ingredients to consider...

SALT

Babies and children shouldn't eat too much salt as it isn't good for their kidneys. Therefore avoid adding salt to baby's meals, or adding it to pasta or vegetable cooking water. Per day:

- **Babies under 12 months** should have less than 1g of salt (0.4g of sodium).

- **Toddlers aged 1–3 years** can have a maximum of 2g of salt (0.8g of sodium).

- **Children aged 4–6 years** can have a maximum of 3g of salt (1.2g of sodium).

- **Children aged 7–10 years** can have a maximum of 5g of salt (2g of sodium).

- **Children aged 11 years to adulthood** can have a maximum of 6g of salt (2.4g of sodium).

To put that into relative terms, a slice of shop-bought medium white bread contains on average 0.4g of salt. So when you're feeding baby, keep a rough calculation in your head of what they have eaten that day (better yet, glance at your meal plan!). But take note, even though you may serve 1 slice of toast to baby, they may not eat it all. Remember that these are guidelines. It's good practice to look at baby's intake across the whole week rather than each meal.

Reducing the amount of salt in your family meals is important for your whole family's health, however this does not have to reduce the flavour. All of the What Mummy Makes recipes have been developed with flavour in mind, without needing additional salt, but if your preference is for saltier tastes, feel free to season your own plate at the table. Remember, this preference is learnt over time, so if you find a need to add extra seasoning, that doesn't mean baby will too.

SUGAR

Keep sugar intake to a minimum so that a sweet preference does not develop and to maintain oral health.

SATURATED FAT

Babies and young children need plenty of fat in their diet as they use up lots of energy growing, learning and being active, so choose full-fat versions of dairy products. However, do be mindful to limit your child's intake of saturated fat in foods like cakes and deep-fried foods.

WHOLE NUTS

Avoid serving whole nuts to children under the age of 5 as this can be a choking hazard. Instead, opt for finely crushed nuts or nut butters like peanut or cashew butter.

RAW EGGS

From 6 months you can serve eggs to baby. In the UK, choose hen's eggs that have the British Lion quality stamp on them, which are safe to serve raw as an ingredient in food like homemade mayonnaise, or lightly cooked like a soft-boiled egg. If you are in doubt, always fully cook the egg until they are solid before serving to baby. This also includes duck, goose or quail's eggs.

HONEY

You **must not** serve honey (raw or cooked) to babies under the age of 12 months as it contains a bacteria that can cause infant botulism.

CERTAIN CHEESE

Cheese is packed full of calcium, protein and vitamins, making it a fantastic food to serve to babies and young children as part of a varied diet. However, it is advised to offer only pasteurized full-fat cheese from the age of 6 months. This includes hard cheese, like Cheddar, cottage cheese and soft cream cheese. There is a risk of the bacteria listeria in soft cheeses like brie, camembert, ripened goat's cheese, blue cheese or cheese made from unpasteurized milk. Listeria can make baby feel very ill so it's best to avoid. However, you can use these cheeses to cook with, as the listeria is killed when cooking.

RICE DRINKS

Babies and young children up to the age of 5 years shouldn't drink rice-based drinks, especially not as a replacement for breast or formula milk, as it contains high levels of arsenic. Babies are fine to eat rice as the levels are monitored in the EU for rice and rice-based products.

FISH AND SHELLFISH

Avoid shark, swordfish and marlin as the high levels of mercury found in them can affect the development of baby's nervous system. Always fully cook shellfish such as mussels, oysters and clams to avoid the risk of food poisoning.

HOW TO CUT AND SERVE FOOD FOR BABY

Eating the same meal together has vast benefits, but it's easier for baby to explore the same food as you if it's served appropriately for their age.

The general rule of thumb is to serve all foods in long finger strips. This is so that baby can grip the food easily in their fist and bring it to their mouth, helping them to explore the flavour and texture independently.

A few examples:

- **Toast** – cut into strips

- **Cooked meat** – cut into strips approximately 1cm (½in) wide, across the grain so it separates easily

- **Hard-boiled eggs** – quarter lengthways

- **Satsumas** – peel and slice across the segments so that the rings separate into little chunks. Keep in whole rings when serving to baby

- **Bananas** – to avoid slippery banana when serving to baby, peel it, then gently press your finger down the centre. You will feel the banana naturally separate into three equal sections, which aren't slippery and are the perfect finger strips for baby to hold. Trust me, it works!

- **Sweetcorn** – corn kernels can be served as is, or whole corn on the cobs can be sliced into 2.5cm (1in) rounds once cooked so baby can feed themselves

- **Avocado** – cut into wedges (for younger babies, leave some of the skin on to aid with grip)

- **Pasta** – choose a large long pasta shape like rigatoni or fusilli spirals so it's easier for baby to grip and feed themselves

- **Pomegranate** – the seeds can be served as is from 6 months as they are too small to be a choking hazard

Small foods like peas, sweetcorn and pomegranate are a fab food to serve to babies who are learning to develop their pincer grip at around the age of 7–9 months.

Look at the quick-grab snacks on page 74 for examples.

STARTING FROM DAY ONE OF WEANING

Once your little one is sitting up unaided, able to coordinate their hands to their mouth, and able to swallow food rather than spit it out, they are ready to wean onto solid food. This will happen around the age of 6 months.

Before you get stuck into all the tasty family meals from What Mummy Makes, it is advised to start with single vegetables for a week or two to gently ease baby onto solid foods. Focus on bitter greens like broccoli or courgette (zucchini) so that baby is exposed to these flavours from the beginning. Breast and formula milk are naturally sweet, so the trick with weaning is to introduce a wide variety of tastes from the start so this preference for sweet tastes doesn't take hold.

You can serve veggies as a purée or finger food, and studies show that offering a mixture of both from the beginning will help your little one get used to a wide variety of textures.

Gently steam or boil the veg until it can be squashed easily between your fingers. You can then cut into finger strips or mash/blend for baby. Once you feel your little one is taking to solids (they probably still won't be swallowing much for a good few weeks), you can move on to all the meal ideas from What Mummy Makes, serving each dish appropriately for your baby's age and eating together to encourage foodie learning.

For much more information on how to start weaning, along with advice on choking, introducing allergens, portion sizes, eating environments and tackling fussy behaviours, head to the *What Mummy Makes: Cook just once for you and your baby* cookbook.

BUILD THE PERFECT PLATE

When planning a meal, try to construct each plate so that it includes a portion of protein like meat, lentils, fish and chickpeas; carbohydrates like pasta or potatoes; and plenty of vegetables and fruit. Ensure you include plenty of dairy into your family's diet for the benefits of added protein, calcium and essential nutrients (if you're dairy free, try to choose fortified substitutes). This can be in the form of yogurt with breakfast or as a dip for savoury meals. Or, add milk to foods as an ingredient along with cheese and fortified plant-based alternatives.

Try to ensure you a little healthy fat each day too. This can come from sources like nuts (serve in nut butter or well-ground form to children under 5), oily fish, avocados, or olive, rapeseed and other seed oils.

Use this handy chart as a rough guide to help you build a balanced meal for your family. It's good practice to serve your little ones the following each day: 5 helpings of fruit and vegetables, 2–3 helpings of protein-rich food, and 2–3 helpings of dairy. Don't worry if they don't eat it all – exposure is key!

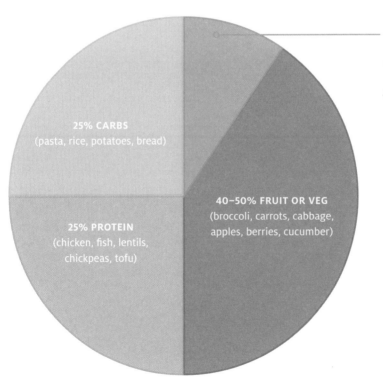

10% DAIRY
(yogurt, cheese and milk as an ingredient for solid foods, in addition to the amount of milk little ones should be having in relation to their age)

25% CARBS
(pasta, rice, potatoes, bread)

40–50% FRUIT OR VEG
(broccoli, carrots, cabbage, apples, berries, cucumber)

25% PROTEIN
(chicken, fish, lentils, chickpeas, tofu)

HERO PANTRY STAPLES

Everyday kitchen staples may sit in your cupboards for a few months waiting to be used. I like to stock up regularly on all of these items so if I go off meal plan, I can definitely whip up a quick and nutritious meal at a moment's notice. Keep track of what you have in on pages 92–93.

STORE CUPBOARD

- Low-salt stock cubes – chicken, beef and vegetable
- Worcestershire sauce
- Low-salt soy sauce
- Sunflower oil
- Garlic-infused olive oil
- Olive or coconut oil cooking spray
- Sesame oil
- Coconut oil
- Red wine vinegar
- Tomato purée (paste)
- Dried pasta – in a variety of shapes: spirali, rigatoni, ditali, macaroni, fusilli lunghi, orzo and fusilli corti buco are a few of my favourites
- Dried uncooked rice
- Packets of ready-cooked mixed grains or rice – unsalted and unflavoured
- Dried couscous
- Breadcrumbs – panko and plain
- Rolled (old-fashioned) porridge oats
- Eggs
- Brown and red onions
- White potatoes
- Sweet potatoes
- Garlic bulbs
- Coconut milk
- Canned tuna in spring water
- Unsweetened canned sweetcorn
- Canned chopped tomatoes – chunky and fine
- Tomato passata
- Variety of canned beans – like kidney, cannellini and haricot (navy beans) – always buy beans with no added salt
- Canned chickpeas (garbanzo beans) in water
- White sliced bread
- Tortilla wraps
- Crumpets
- Flours – plain (all-purpose), self-raising and cornflour (cornstarch)
- Baking powder
- Cocoa powder
- Golden caster (superfine) sugar
- Honey (do not serve honey to babies under 12 months)
- Maple syrup
- Pure vanilla extract (not essence)
- Ground flaxseed
- Chia seeds
- Sesame seeds
- Poppy seeds
- Seedless raisins
- Unsweetened desiccated (dried shredded) coconut
- Peanut butter (100% nuts with no palm oil)
- Canned fruit in juice (not syrup) – peaches, pears, prunes
- Apple purée pouches – 100% apple (found in the baby food aisle)

SPICES & DRIED HERBS
- Mild garam masala
- Mild curry powder
- Garlic granules
- Onion granules
- Smoked paprika
- Ground cumin
- Ground cinnamon
- Ground ginger
- Ground mixed spice
- Mixed dried herbs
- Black pepper mill

FRIDGE
- Full-fat Greek-style yogurt
- Cheddar cheese – medium or strong
- Full-fat cream cheese
- Full-fat (whole) milk
- Unsalted butter
- Ready-rolled puff pastry
- Broccoli
- Carrots
- Chives
- Cucumber
- Courgettes (zucchini)
- Berries, usually raspberries and blueberries
- Ketchup with no added sugar or salt

FRUIT BOWL
- Bananas
- Apples
- Satsumas
- Lemons
- Kiwis

FROZEN
- Frozen spinach cubes (chopped if possible)
- Frozen mixed veg
- Frozen broccoli
- Frozen peas
- Frozen berries

WHAT KITCHEN EQUIPMENT IS REALLY USEFUL?

It would be so easy for me to write an extensive list of all the useless gadgets I own, but honestly, I use them once or twice a year. Here's what comes out on a regular basis and what I feel are essential tools to have in the kitchen.

POTS AND PANS

- Small milk saucepan
- Medium high-sided, non-stick saucepan
- Large low-sided, non-stick frying pan
- Large lidded sauté pan
- High-sided ovenproof casserole dish

- Low-sided baking dish – ceramic or glass
- Large baking trays (at least one as large as your oven can hold)
- Non-stick 12-hole muffin tray
- Non-stick 24-hole mini muffin tray
- 900g (2lb) non-stick loaf tin

UTENSILS

- Large, very sharp slicing knife with a sturdy blade that feels comfortable for you
- Small paring knife
- Small serrated knife
- Large serrated bread knife
- Vegetable peeler
- Measuring spoons
- Dinner forks, for mashing
- Box grater with coarse and fine grating surfaces
- Potato masher
- Rubber/nylon firm spatula
- Rubber/nylon firm fish slice

- Cooking tongs
- Stainless steel wire skimmer spoon (use this for moving pasta from the pot to the sauce)
- Large ladle
- Can opener
- Pizza cutter
- Rubber/nylon whisk suitable for use with non-stick pans
- Pastry brush
- Kitchen scissors
- Garlic crusher
- Wooden spoons

ELECTRICALS

- Hand stick blender
- Food processor
- Fan-assisted electric oven
- Kettle
- Microwave

EXTRAS

- A good heavy chopping board
- An egg pricker (not necessary but I use it all the time!)
- Mixing bowls in a range of sizes – from small for whipping up quick dips to large bowls for cake and fritter batters
- Kitchen scales
- Colander
- Sieve (strainer)
- Cooling rack
- Rolling pin
- Non-stick baking paper
- Non-stick kitchen foil
- Cookie cutters

MAKING YOUR LEFTOVERS DELICIOUS!

I'm either hopeless for cooking far too much, or I deliberately make loads so we have plenty for the next day! Sometimes leftovers can be just as delicious the following day when you follow some of my tips and tricks to transform them into a whole new meal.

Leftover cold saucy foods, like curry or pasta sauce, are delicious wrapped up in pastry and baked. Either make little hand pies (see page 56) or, If you have plenty of your leftover, fill a baking dish and top with puff or short-crust pastry. Brush a little egg wash over the pastry for colour and sprinkle the top with seeds, like poppy or onion seeds, for extra flavour. Bake in a hot oven 220ºC fan (240ºC/475ºF/Gas 9) until the pastry has puffed up and is golden, and the inside is piping hot all the way through. Depending on the size of your baking dish, this can take 20–35 minutes.

Turn yesterday's roast chicken into a curry with spices and coconut milk. Try the What Mummy Makes my first curry recipe as a base and add the leftover meat in the last 10 minutes of cooking to ensure it's piping hot all the way through without drying out.

Leftover roast pork or beef is really yummy cut into small chunks, popped in a hot frying pan with a little garlic-infused olive oil and fried until crispy. Then, towards the end of cooking, add a sprinkle of smoked paprika, ground cumin, garlic granules and mixed dried herbs. Stuff between a mini tortilla wrap or fill a warm pitta bread along with some salad and garlicky yogurt – YUM!

Leftover steamed or boiled veg is great chopped up a little and added to pasta sauces. Or roast it with a little garlic-infused olive oil and your favourite spices until charred on the edges to breathe a new lease of life into those greens!

Try the leftover mashed potato cakes on page 42, the leftover pasta bake on page 38, and the leftover porridge bars on page 68 to use up the foods that are most commonly cooked in excess.

Leftover hot cross buns or croissants that are turning stale make the most delicious eggy bread (see page 27) or bread and butter pudding (see page 80)!

The general rule to reheating leftovers is to ensure that they are piping hot all the way through and, if possible, add in some extra flavour and texture to zing up the meal so you don't feel like you're eating the same meal again. Get creative: it's really hard to go wrong!

Leftovers from baby's plate must not be stored overnight as the bacteria from their saliva can cause the food to have unsafe bacteria levels if stored for a long period. However, a couple of hours is OK.

100 Foods Challenge

Use this space to jot down the first 100 foods your baby has tried since they started weaning, for example strawberries, toast, pasta, etc. See if you can fill the list by their 1st birthday!

IS YOUR CHILD PAST WEANING AGE?
Jot down all the meals your family really enjoy so you can reference back when planning. But remember to offer foods your little ones are still learning to love!

1 ....
2 ....
3 ....
4 ....
5 ....
6 ....
7 ....
8 ....
9 ....
10 ....
11 ....
12 ....
13 ....
14 ....
15 ....
16 ....
17 ....
18 ....
19 ....
20 ....
21 ....
22 ....

23 ....
24 ....
25 ....
26 ....
27 ....
28 ....
29 ....
30 ....
31 ....
32 ....
33 ....
34 ....
35 ....
36 ....
37 ....
38 ....
39 ....
40 ....
41 ....
42 ....
43 ....
44 ....

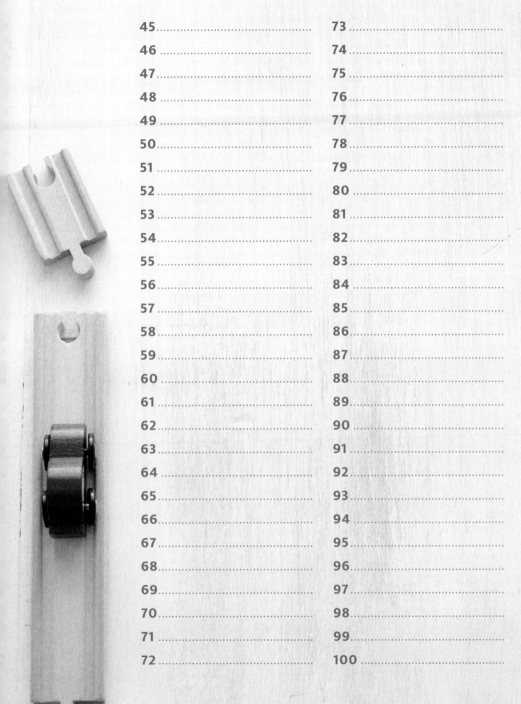

45 ....
46 ....
47 ....
48 ....
49 ....
50 ....
51 ....
52 ....
53 ....
54 ....
55 ....
56 ....
57 ....
58 ....
59 ....
60 ....
61 ....
62 ....
63 ....
64 ....
65 ....
66 ....
67 ....
68 ....
69 ....
70 ....
71 ....
72 ....

73 ....
74 ....
75 ....
76 ....
77 ....
78 ....
79 ....
80 ....
81 ....
82 ....
83 ....
84 ....
85 ....
86 ....
87 ....
88 ....
89 ....
90 ....
91 ....
92 ....
93 ....
94 ....
95 ....
96 ....
97 ....
98 ....
99 ....
100 ....

Breakfast

NOTE
Texturally, babies from
6 months of age can eat
porridge as it is made here.
However, if you wish, you can
blitz the oats before cooking,
or blend the porridge once
made for a smooth
consistency.

PLENTIFUL PORRIDGE

Porridge is the ultimate breakfast fast food. It's super healthy and easy to cram in all those extra nutrients. Follow this easy, no scales method for cooking a simple porridge base. You can switch up the flavour using different milks, as well as adding any extras you fancy, either to the pan, or serve on top in the bowl.

🍴 2 adults and 1 little

⏱ 10 minutes

1 regular mug rolled (old-fashioned) porridge oats*

2 regular mugs full-fat (whole) or plant-based milk of your choice* (see note below)

EXTRAS THAT ARE BEST COOKED INTO THE PORRIDGE

handful of grated carrot or courgette (zucchini)

1 tsp pure vanilla extract

1 tsp ground cinnamon

small handful of seedless raisins

1 tbsp cocoa powder (if using cocoa, it's best to add a sweet fruit, like banana, too to balance the bitterness)

EXTRAS THAT CAN BE COOKED IN OR SERVED ON TOP

2 tbsp nut butters, such as 100% peanut, almond or cashew

1 apple, grated

½ pineapple, grated

1 large banana, mashed or sliced

handful of fresh or frozen berries (blueberries turn the porridge violet, raspberries, pink, and blackberries mean purple porridge)

handful of ripe plums/ apricots/nectarines/ peaches, thinly sliced, grated or mashed

1 avocado, mashed or sliced

1 tbsp crushed nuts

1 mango, puréed or sliced

2 tbsp desiccated (dried shredded) coconut

1 tbsp chia, flax, poppy or sesame seeds

drizzle of honey (only for children over the age of 12 months) or maple syrup

Fill up the mug with oats and pour into a saucepan. Then fill up the same mug (to the same level as the oats) with your choice of milk and add to the pan; do this twice so you have a 2:1 ratio of milk to oats.

Now add any optional extras and cook on a medium–high heat, stirring very often, for around 4 minutes or until the porridge has thickened to your desired consistency. If it's thickening too much, add a splash more milk, or if you feel it's too thin, add a small handful of extra oats and cook until thickened.

Serve with any optional extras.

Leftover porridge will last in the fridge for a couple of days or freeze in portions up to 3 months. To reheat, add an extra splash of milk and heat in the microwave or in a saucepan until piping hot.

TOP TIP

If you have a hungry little one waiting for their brekkie, serve their porridge on a plate so that it cools much more quickly. Adding frozen fruit on top also speeds up the cooling process, and the warm porridge defrosts the fruit.

If you are using a plant-based milk option, try to use a fortified product where possible. There is a great selection of dairy-free alternatives, including soy, oat, pea and coconut milk, as well as nut milks such as almond, cashew and hazelnut.

SWEET BREAKFAST PINWHEELS

A take on a Danish cinnamon swirl pastry, this version is packed with naturally sweet apples and banana. Whip up a batch to have warm for breakfast, and pop the rest in the freezer to enjoy another day.

 12 pinwheels
⏱ 25 minutes

1 large banana
1 red eating apple
1 heaped tbsp ground
  almonds (see note)
1 heaped tsp ground
  cinnamon
1 tsp pure vanilla extract
1 x 375g (13oz) sheet of
  ready-rolled puff
  pastry*

Preheat the oven to 200ºC fan (220ºC/425ºF/Gas 7) and line a baking tray with non-stick baking paper.

Put the banana in a flat-bottomed bowl and mash well with the back of a fork. Grate the apple: no need to remove the skin, but grate around the central core and discard it. Add the apple pulp to the banana, along with the ground almonds, cinnamon and vanilla extract and give it all a good stir.

Unroll the puff pastry and spoon on the banana mix. Using the back of a tablespoon, evenly spread the mixture from edge to edge. Starting at one of the short ends, roll up the pastry into a sausage shape. Use a serrated knife to cut the roll into 12 slices.

Lay each pinwheel onto the lined baking tray, cut side down, so that you see the lovely spiral pattern on top. Bake for 15–20 minutes, or until the pastry is puffed up and golden.

These pinwheels will keep for 3 days in the fridge; reheat for 5 minutes in a hot oven. Or freeze for up to 3 months and cook them from frozen at 180ºC fan (200ºC/400ºF/Gas 6) for 10 minutes, or until piping hot all the way through.

NOTES ABOUT NUTS

If you have a nut allergy, you can omit the ground almonds, but ensure you squeeze out the juice from the grated apples before mixing with the rest of the ingredients, otherwise it'll result in soggy pastry.

CHEESY COURGETTE SCONE FINGERS

For breakfast, lunch or a snack, these veg-packed scones will be a winner all round.

🍴 12 fingers

⏱ 25 minutes

60ml (2fl oz) full fat (whole) milk or plant-based alternative*

2 medium eggs or an additional 115ml (3¾fl oz) milk*

300g (10½oz) self-raising flour, plus extra for dusting

50g (1¾oz) cold unsalted butter or dairy-free alternative*

½ tsp mustard powder (optional)

130g (4½oz) Cheddar cheese or plant-based alternative*, grated

1 large or 2 small courgettes (zucchini)

1 tbsp poppy seeds (optional)

Preheat the oven to 200°C fan (220°C/425°F/Gas 7) and line a large baking tray with non-stick baking paper.

Measure the milk and eggs into a jug and whisk together, then set aside.

Put the flour, butter and mustard (if using) into a large bowl and, using the tips of your fingers, rub the butter into the flour until it resembles breadcrumbs. Shaking the bowl gently will bring any large lumps of butter to the surface.

Grate the courgette using a box grater, then, taking small handfuls at a time, cup the courgette pulp in your hands and squeeze out the juice before adding to the flour; ensure that you remove as much moisture as you can, as too much liquid will result in soggy scones.

Add the grated cheese to the courgette and flour mix, and give it all a good stir so everything is coated well in flour.

Make a well in the centre, and pour in the milk and egg mixture, reserving a little to brush on the top of the scone. Using a round-ended dinner knife, mix together in a cutting motion, spinning the bowl as you go. Quickly mix the dough together, but be sure not to overwork it as this will result in chewy flat scones.

As you see the mix coming together, tip out onto a floured work surface and quickly bring it together to form a ball. Using your hands, gently pat down into a flat, rough rectangle shape around 2cm (¾in) thick. Using a knife, cut into 12 strips, approx 10cm (4in) long and 2.5cm (1in) wide, then transfer to the lined baking tray.

Brush the tops with the remaining milk and egg mixture, ensuring no liquid spills down the sides as this stops a high rise. Sprinkle over the poppy seeds before popping in the oven to bake for 10–12 minutes until puffed up and golden on top.

For little ones, cut the fingers in half so they're easier to hold, and serve with yogurt for dunking and fresh fruit on the side.

Store in an airtight container in the fridge for up to a week, or freeze for 3 months.

NOTE
These scones
go really well with
What Mummy Makes
quick no-sugar summer
fruits jam made with
chia seeds.

bamboo
bamboo

BAKEWELL EGGY BREAD

Transform the humble piece of bread into a breakfast you can't resist. With almond flavours inspired by a Bakewell tart, this brekkie is a great way to add nutrient-rich nuts into your little one's diet.

🍴 1 adult and 1 little
⏲ 10 minutes

2 medium eggs
2 tsp almond extract
1 tbsp ground almonds
tiny knob of unsalted
    butter or sunflower
    oil*, for frying
2 slices of your favourite
    bread*
handful of fresh
    raspberries, mashed
    with the back of a fork
Greek-style yogurt of
    your choice*, to serve

Put the eggs, almond extract and ground almonds into a large flat-bottomed bowl and whisk together well.

Set a large non-stick frying pan over a medium heat, add the butter and let it melt while the pan warms up.

Meanwhile, one at a time, dip the bread slices into the egg mixture and soak for 20 seconds on each side until they're completely coated and you can see no dry bread at all.

Add the soaked bread to the now-hot frying pan and cook for about 2 minutes on each side. If there is a small amount of egg mixture left in the bowl, spoon it on top of the eggy breads before flipping over.

Once golden in colour, remove the eggy bread from the pan and dab with paper towels to soak up any excess butter. Cut the slices into halves, quarters or strips.

Mix the mashed raspberries into some yogurt for dipping and serve with the eggy bread.

Eggy bread will keep in an airtight container in the fridge for 2 days or up to 3 months in the freezer. Reheat in the microwave for a minute, or in a frying pan or the oven for a couple of minutes until piping hot throughout.

A NOTE ABOUT BREAD
White bread is best for little tummies as too many wholegrain (whole-wheat) foods fill them up too quickly, resulting in less of an appetite for a varied and balanced diet. You can use gluten-free bread if you wish.

CINNAMON APPLE PANCAKES WITH NUTTY YOGURT

The nutty yogurt in this breakfast is delicious on its own, but when you pair it with comforting fruity pancakes, it's a taste sensation!

🍴 15 pancakes
🕑 20 minutes

2 eating apples
1 tsp ground cinnamon
130g (4½oz) self-raising
    flour
1 tsp baking powder
180ml (6fl oz) full-fat
    (whole) milk or
    plant-based
    alternative*
2 medium eggs
    or 2 chia eggs*
    (see below)

NUTTY YOGURT
4 tbsp yogurt or
    plant-based
    alternative*
1 heaped tbsp ground
    almonds
2 tsp smooth nut butter
    (100% peanut or
    almond are best)
2 tsp maple syrup
    (optional)

Using a box grater, coarsely grate the unpeeled apples on all sides so you are left with a square core to discard.

Put the apple in a large bowl with the rest of the pancake ingredients and stir well to combine.

Set a large, non-stick frying pan over low–medium heat. In batches, scoop heaped tablespoons of the batter into the preheated pan, shaping into circles as the batter meets the pan. Cook for 1–2 minutes. Once you see bubbles forming, they're ready to flip with a thin rubber spatula. Cook for a further 2 minutes, or until the pancakes are cooked through. Reduce the heat if the outsides are browning too quickly before the insides have had a chance to cook. Repeat until all the batter is used up.

Meanwhile, make the nutty yogurt by mixing all the ingredients together. Set aside until the pancakes are ready.

To serve, cut the pancakes into finger strips for baby and serve with nutty yogurt for dipping. And for those who have mastered using cutlery, stack them high and serve with the yogurt on top.

Store the pancakes in an airtight container in the fridge for 2 days or for up to 3 months in the freezer. Store the nutty yogurt for 2 days in the fridge. It's best to avoid freezing the yogurt as the texture will change once defrosted.

COOK FROM FROZEN
When freezing pancakes, store them with a piece of baking paper between each pancake to avoid them sticking together. Reheat them in the toaster, microwave or frying pan until hot.

CHIA EGGS
To make a chia egg substitute for hens' eggs, mix 1 tbsp chia seeds with 2½ tbsp warm water per 1 egg required. Scale up as necessary: so for 2 eggs, use 2 tbsp chia seeds and 5 tbsp warm water, and so on. Set the chia egg mixture aside for 10 minutes before using. This can also be done with ground flaxseed.

BLUEBERRY BREAKFAST COBBLER

Naturally sweet and soft berries topped with an oaty cake-like topping. So tasty, you can enjoy this fruity cobbler as a warming breakfast or a dessert.

🍽 3 adults and 2 littles

⏱ 30 minutes

FRUITY FILLING

400g (14oz) bag of
    frozen blueberries
2 medium bananas
2 tsp pure vanilla extract
1 tbsp cornflour
    (cornstarch)

COBBLER TOPPING

120g (4¼oz) self-raising
    flour*
40g (14oz) rolled
    (old-fashioned) oats*
1 tsp baking powder
120ml (4fl oz) full-fat
    (whole) milk or
    plant-based
    alternative*
1 heaped tsp ground
    cinnamon
1 medium egg or 1 chia
    egg (see page 28)*
1 tbsp demerara
    (turbinado) sugar
    (optional)
yogurt of your choice*,
    to serve

Preheat the oven to 220°C fan (240°C/475°F/Gas 8).

Pop the bag of frozen blueberries in the microwave. Heat on full power for 1 minute 30 seconds to defrost a little; this will help the cobbler bake faster. (Ensure the bag is microwave safe. If you're unsure, decant the fruit into a microwaveable bowl first.)

Meanwhile, add the bananas to a large, flat-bottomed mixing bowl and mash them with the back of a spoon. Add the microwaved blueberries to the banana, along with the vanilla, cornflour and 2 tbsp cold water, and mix well.

To make the topping, put all the ingredients, except the sugar, into a bowl and mix well. It will create a soft batter.

Divide the fruit mixture between 4 large ramekins. Use two tablespoons to spoon a few mounds of the batter onto each pudding, leaving gaps for the fruit to bubble up, which gives the "cobbled" effect.

Place the ramekins on a baking sheet and sprinkle each with a tiny amount of sugar – this is optional but it does give a lovely crust on top. Pop in the oven for 20–25 minutes or until the fruit is bubbling and the topping has cooked all the way through.

Once ready, allow to stand for a minute before serving with yogurt. To serve to little ones, decant the cobbler into a chilled bowl to help it cool more quickly and save their little fingers on the hot ramekin.

Leftovers will keep in an airtight container for a couple of days in the fridge, or for 2 months in the freezer. Defrost completely, then reheat in the oven for 10 minutes, or until piping hot.

TOP TIPS

You can use fresh berries, but skip the microwave step if you do.

You can use one large baking dish (1.3 litre/1¼ quart) to cook the cobbler in, but you'll need to increase the cooking time by 10–15 minutes to ensure the topping cooks all the way through.

DIPPY EGGS WITH CHEESY CRUMPET SOLDIERS

With or without the dippy egg, these gloriously cheesy crumpets are so moreish: the perfect weekend treat.

🍴 1 adult and 1 little
⏱ 10 minutes

30g (1oz) cream cheese
3 crumpets
35g (1¼oz) Cheddar cheese, grated
3 large free-range British lion-stamped hens' eggs at room temperature (see page 6 and tip below)

Bring a saucepan of water to a rolling boil, and preheat the oven to 200°C fan (220°C/425°F/Gas 7).

Spread 1 tbsp, about 10g (⅓oz) of the cream cheese on each crumpet. Top with a little grated cheese, then pop the loaded crumpets onto a baking tray lined with non-stick foil.

Using a slotted spoon, all at once, lower the eggs into the water and quickly set your timer to 5 minutes.

Now, pop the crumpets in the oven. This is a great time to prepare some fruit to have on the side, and get all the plates together.

Remove the eggs from the pan and place in a bowl.

Check the crumpets: if the cheese has melted and turned a dark brown colour, they're ready. Remove from the oven.

Run baby's egg under a cold tap so it's cool enough to handle. Gently peel, being careful to avoid breaking the white open, then pop into a small bowl or onto a baby plate. Using a spoon, gently break up the egg so the yolk runs out.

Slice the crumpets into 1.5cm (⅝in) wide fingers and serve alongside the egg for dunking.

TIP
If you have a small dressmaker's needle, or an egg pricker, prick a small hole in the egg shells before boiling; this prevents the shell cracking when cooking.

Lunch

SPICED CARROT SHEET-PAN FRITTERS

EF* V Vg* DF*

Start the week with a little spice! Mild in heat but packed full of flavour, these carrot fritters are great to fill up the freezer and pull out for quick lunches, picnics or snacks in a hurry.

🍴 12–15 fritters
⏲ 25 minutes

2 carrots, coarsely grated
80g (2½oz) Cheddar
    cheese or plant-based
    alternative*, grated
1 tsp garlic granules or
    1 garlic clove, minced
½ tsp ground cumin
1 tsp smoked paprika
1 tsp garam masala

1 tsp baking powder
100g (3½oz) self-raising
    flour
100ml (3½fl oz) full-fat
    (whole) milk or
    plant-based
    alternative*
2 medium eggs or 2 chia
    eggs (see page 28)*

Preheat the oven to 200°C fan (220°C/425°F/Gas 7) and line a shallow-sided metal baking tray with non-stick baking paper.

Mix all the ingredients together, then spread the batter onto the tray so it is about 1cm (½in) thick. If your baking tray is too large, just form the batter into a smaller bake; the shape will hold, so just ensure the thickness is correct.

Bake in the preheated oven for 15–20 minutes until puffed up and golden on top.

Using a pizza cutter, cut into squares (or finger strips if serving to baby). Serve with a picky salad and some Greek-style yogurt for dipping.

These fritters will keep in the fridge for 2 days, or top up your freezer stash for up to 3 months. Either warm up from frozen in the microwave, or allow to defrost completely at room temperature and reheat in the oven for 5 minutes until piping hot inside.

TIP
You can use pretty
much any veg you like
to make these fritters
- try courgette or
sweetcorn.

SALMON AND BROCCOLI PASTA BAKE

Use up your pea pasta leftovers (see page 53) to create a whole new delicious meal. Or you can use any creamy pasta leftovers to make the dish. If you don't have any leftovers, just whip up a little batch of cheese sauce and stir it through freshly cooked pasta.

🍴 2 adults and 1 little
(depending on
how much pasta
leftovers you have)

⏲ 30 minutes

150g (5½oz) broccoli
florets
600–800g (1lb 5oz–
1lb 12oz) leftover
pea pasta (see
page 53)
2–3 skinless salmon fillets
3 tbsp full-fat (whole)
milk or plant-based
alternative*
50g (1¾oz) Cheddar
cheese or plant-based
alternative*, grated
freshly ground black
pepper

Preheat the oven to 200°C fan (220°C/425°F/Gas 7).

Steam the broccoli florets in a strainer set over a pan of simmering water, or in the microwave on high for 4 minutes.

Meanwhile, tip the leftover cold pasta into an ovenproof dish big enough that the pasta sits snuggly inside.

Cut the salmon fillets, widthways, into 1.5cm (⅝in) slices. Add to the pasta, along with the milk and the now-cooked and drained broccoli. Gently stir, then spread the mixture into all corners of the oven dish.

Sprinkle with the grated cheese and give the dish a good grinding of black pepper. Bake for 15–20 minutes until the top is golden and the salmon is cooked through.

MAKE IT GLUTEN-FREE!

There are lots of gluten-free pasta options available, like chickpea or lentil pasta. They are also great for getting in extra nutrients like protein! If you're serving to young babies, you may need to cook for longer than the packet advises to ensure it's soft enough for baby to enjoy.

TIP
These tuna straws are
really delicious cold, so this
recipe is great to follow when
you're whipping up snacks for
during the week, or for a delicious
picnic with your family. They
would also be perfect
for a celebration party
buffet too!

TUNA AND SWEETCORN CHEESE STRAWS

A deliciously savoury combination of tuna and sweetcorn stuffed between gloriously flaky puff pastry. They are just the perfect balance between soft centre and crispy outside bits! I guarantee you won't be able to just have one!

🍴 14 straws
⏱ 25 minutes

1 can tuna in spring water
55g (2oz) Cheddar cheese
  or plant-based
  alternative*, grated
120g (4¼oz) canned
  sweetcorn, drained
65g (2¼oz) soft cream
  cheese or dairy-free
  alternative*
1 x 375g (13oz) sheet of
  ready-rolled puff pastry
1 small egg, or 1½ tbsp
  milk of your choice*
freshly ground black
  pepper

SOUR CREAM
AND CHIVE DIP
3 tbsp sour cream* (see
  note below)
1 tbsp thick Greek-style
  yogurt*
1 tbsp finely chopped
  chives
½ garlic clove, crushed

Preheat the oven to 200°C fan (220°C/425°F/Gas 7) and line a large baking tray with non-stick baking paper.

Drain the tuna well and put it in a bowl with the Cheddar, sweetcorn, cream cheese, and a generous grinding of black pepper. Give it all a good mix until well combined.

Unroll the pastry and lay it out landscape format, with a long edge in front of you. Spread the tuna mixture over the top half of the pastry. Fold up the clean half of the pastry closest to you by flipping it over the top half to cover the tuna filling and press it into the mixture, leaving you with a tuna pastry sandwich.

Cut the folded pastry widthways into 14 strips, each about 2.5cm (1in) thick. One at a time, hold each strip by the ends and twist your hands in opposite directions to twist the pastry, then place on the prepared baking tray.

Whisk the egg and, using a pastry brush, apply an egg wash onto the exposed pastry. Pop in the oven for 15–20 minutes.

While the straws bake, make up the dip by mixing all the ingredients together and setting aside. Let it sit for at least 10 minutes for all the flavours to mingle.

The straws are done when they have taken on a lovely brown colour, the pastry looks firm and flaky, and they are piping hot throughout. Serve the straws with the dip and a picky salad.

Leftovers can be kept in the fridge for 2 days and reheated in the oven. Or you can freeze for up to 2 months. From frozen, pop the straws in the oven at 180°C fan (200°C/400°F/Gas 6) for 10–15 minutes, or until piping hot all the way through.

DAIRY-FREE DIPPING
To make the dip dairy-free, switch the sour cream and Greek-style yogurt for 4 tbsp thick dairy-free yogurt.

LEFTOVER MASHED POTATO CAKES

Bring leftover mashed potato back to new life with these soft and oozy little savoury cakes. They are really yummy served with a fried egg for dunking and, if your little ones are old enough, a few rashers of bacon.

8 potato cakes
10 minutes

100g (3½oz) frozen peas
400g (14oz) cold mashed
   potato*
110g (3¾oz) plain
   (all-purpose) flour
1 tsp baking powder
1 tsp garlic granules
½ tsp onion granules
60g (2oz) Cheddar
   cheese, finely grated
   (optional*)
about 50g (1¾oz)
   chopped ham or crispy
   bacon (optional* –
   reduce the quantity if
   your little one is under
   1 year)
sunflower oil, for frying
freshly ground black
   pepper

Put the peas in a microwaveable bowl, cover and heat on high power for 90 seconds to defrost.

Meanwhile, measure the rest of the ingredients into a mixing bowl. Once the peas are defrosted, run under cold water, drain and add to the mixing bowl. Give everything a good stir to combine.

Divide the mixture evenly into 8 portions, and form each one into a small patty shape. Set a frying pan over medium–high heat and add a little oil to the pan. Fry the patties for 2 or so minutes on each side, or until the outsides have browned well and the insides are piping hot.

Cut the cakes into finger strips or quarters to serve to baby – these cakes are really soft, so smaller pieces will be easier for baby to manage.

TOP TIPS

If you used lots of milk and butter to make the original mashed potato, you may need to add a touch more flour if you feel the potato cake mixture is too loose to shape.

If your child follows a dairy-free or vegan diet, ensure that the leftover mashed potato uses dairy-free alternatives.

TIP
If you don't have as much leftover mash as the recipe states, weigh what you have and reduce the rest of the ingredients accordingly.

SMOKY COURGETTE AND CHICKPEA MUFFINS

Protein-packed chickpeas give these muffins a fab variety in texture. Super-soft courgettes paired with crushed chickpeas add a teeny amount of bite, which make these savoury muffins so irresistible. Consistently offering a wide variety of textures to our little ones' diets really helps to reduce fussiness in the long run.

🍴 12 muffins
🕐 25 minutes

400g (14oz) can chickpeas (garbanzo beans), drained
1 large courgette (zucchini)
85g (3oz) unsalted butter or dairy-free spread*, melted, plus optional extra for greasing
90g (3¼oz) Cheddar cheese, grated, or 1 heaped tbsp nutritional yeast*
180g (6¼oz) self-raising flour
1 tsp baking powder
1 heaped tsp smoked paprika
3 medium eggs or 3 chia eggs (see page 28)*
60ml (2fl oz) full-fat (whole) milk or plant-based alternative*
freshly ground black pepper

Preheat the oven to 180°C fan (200°C/400°F/Gas 6) and grease a 12-hole non-stick muffin tray with butter. Alternatively, use non-stick paper cases.

Put the chickpeas into a large mixing bowl and, using the back of a large ladle, roughly mash to break them down a little.

Grate the courgette and squeeze out the juice before adding the pulp to the mixing bowl with the chickpeas. Add all the remaining ingredients and give it a good mix, but be careful not to overwork the batter.

Divide the mixture evenly between the 12 holes of the muffin tray, or the paper cases, and bake for 15–20 minutes until puffed up, golden and smelling delicious. To check if they are cooked all the way through, insert a knife into the thickest part of a muffin and if it comes out clean they are done. Leave the muffins to cool on a wire rack.

Store in an airtight container at room temperature for up to 3 days, or pop in the freezer for 2 months. Defrost and warm up in the microwave or oven. Alternatively, you can let thaw at room temperature and eat cold.

PIZZA EGGY BREAD ROLL-UPS

Wow your family with these gorgeous little mouthfuls – they are so pretty when you cut into them, and make a great finger food for baby. Really yummy made with classic pizza flavourings, you can also add extra fillings to use up what you've got in.

🍴 4 roll-ups

⏱ 15 minutes

3 tbsp tomato purée
  (paste)
½ tsp mixed dried herbs
1 tsp smoked paprika
½ tsp garlic granules or
  1 garlic clove, minced
4 slices of white bread or
  gluten-free bread*
small handful of grated
  Cheddar or mozzarella
  cheese, or plant-based
  alternative*
sunflower oil, for frying
1 large egg

OPTIONAL EXTRA
FILLINGS
(use as many as you like,
  but if using multiple
  fillings use less of each
  to avoid over-filling)
4 slices of ham*
2 tbsp wilted chopped
  spinach (juice
  squeezed out)
½ courgette (zucchini),
  grated and juice
  squeezed out
very thinly sliced
  mushrooms
thinly sliced olives
  (in moderation –
  they're salty)
1 tbsp pesto*

Mix the tomato purée, herbs, paprika, garlic and 3 tbsp water together in a small bowl, then set aside.

Cut the crusts off the bread slices, then roll each piece of bread with a rolling pin on both sides until it's as flat as you can get it.

Spread the tomato sauce edge to edge over each piece of bread. Top with your choice of filling, being careful not to add too much as they won't roll neatly. Add a little cheese, then, from one of the short ends of the bread, roll up each slice as tightly as you can. Leave each roll-up seam-side down so it doesn't unravel.

Set a non-stick frying pan over a medium heat and add a small drizzle of oil. While the pan heats up, whisk the egg in a bowl and add the roll-ups, moving them around to coat all sides. Dip in each end to allow the egg to soak into the exposed spiral.

Add the roll-ups to the pan, seam-side down first to cook the seal shut. Rotate by 90 degrees every 30–60 seconds, cooking on all sides, and don't forget to sear the ends briefly too. It's better to cook these low and slow, to allow the cheese inside to melt before the outside starts to char.

Once cooked, place the roll-ups on a plate lined with paper towels to drain any excess oil. Slice diagonally in half to expose the lovely spiral pattern. Serve with yogurt or ketchup for dipping, with some cucumber sticks and fruit on the side.

Store in the fridge for up to 2 days. Reheat in a pan or pop in the microwave on high for 1 minute, or until piping hot inside.

FREEZER STASH!

You could spend 20 minutes making a big batch of these roll-ups to fill up the freezer. Store with a little baking paper between each one to prevent sticking, then pop into the microwave for 2–3 minutes from frozen, flipping halfway through cooking and ensuring they are piping hot inside.

TIP
Plenty of crusts? Let
them dry out, then blitz
for quick homemade
breadcrumbs.

30-MINUTE SUNDAY ROAST

The week often doesn't feel complete without a Sunday roast to feast on till you pop. But when you have little ones running around, it's hard to find the time to spend hours in the kitchen prepping all the components. Here's roast chicken with roasties, veg, gravy AND yorkshires that you can get ready in just 30 minutes!

🍴 2 adults and 2 littles
⏲ 30 minutes

ROAST CHICKEN
1kg (2¼lb) chicken thighs
1 tsp garlic-infused olive oil
½ large lemon
1 large white onion, cut into wedges (skin on)
1 tsp mixed dried herbs
1 tsp garlic granules
400ml (14fl oz) low-salt chicken stock (from a cube), hot
freshly ground black pepper

ROAST POTATOES
about 1kg (2¼lb) new potatoes
1 tbsp garlic-infused olive oil

YORKSHIRE PUDDINGS
a little sunflower oil
3 medium cold eggs
150ml (5fl oz) full-fat (whole) milk
150g (5½oz) plain (all-purpose) flour

GRAVY
1 tsp cornflour (cornstarch)
1 tbsp low-salt soy sauce
1 tbsp Worcestershire sauce

VEGETABLES
250g (9oz) of your favourite veg, such as peas, broccoli or carrots.

NOTE
You will need an oven with at least three shelves, or multiple trays which will fit snuggly on one shelf. If you're struggling for space, you may need to skip the Yorkshire puddings or swap roasties for mash instead.

Preheat the oven to 220°C fan (240°C/475°F/Gas 9) and drizzle a tiny amount of oil into each hole of a 24-hole mini muffin tray. Pop in the oven to heat up.

Halve any larger potatoes lengthways and put them all in a microwaveable dish. Cover and cook on full power for 4 minutes.

Meanwhile, put the chicken thighs, skin-side up, into a large roasting tray lined with non-stick foil. Pour the hot stock into the tray, then drizzle over the oil and lemon juice, adding the squeezed rind to the tray too. Nestle the onion wedges between the chicken pieces. Add all of the other seasonings, making sure to evenly sprinkle over each piece of chicken.

Put the potatoes onto a separate baking tray. Add the oil and stir to coat, then pop both the potato and chicken trays into the oven for 20–25 minutes.

Now quickly make up the Yorkshire pudding batter by adding all the ingredients to a jug and whisking until smooth. Very carefully remove the hot muffin tray from the oven, shutting the door behind you. Quickly fill each hole three-quarters full and get the tray on the top shelf of the oven as soon as possible to bake for 12–15 minutes. Don't open the door for at least 12 minutes.

While everything roasts, get prepped for the gravy. Add the cornflour to a small bowl with 1 tbsp of water and mix well until you have a smooth, silky slurry. Put a kettle filled with water on to boil and set a small saucepan with a dash of water over a high heat.

Now is a good time to boil your chosen veg for 4–7 minutes, or until tender.

By now the chicken should be cooked through with the skin crispy, the potatoes lovely and golden and the Yorkshire puddings puffed up well. Take everything out of the oven.

Transfer the chicken, onions and lemon rind to a serving dish, then pour the juices from the roasting tray into the hot saucepan, scraping in as much of the crispy chicken pieces as you can – this is where all the flavour is! Add 200ml (7fl oz) of boiled kettle water and the soy and Worcestershire sauces, and bring to the boil. Add the cornflour slurry, stirring continuously for a minute – it should thicken quickly.

To serve a roast dinner to little ones, cut the potatoes in half lengthways, remove the chicken from the bone and tear the Yorkshire pudding up a bit. Soak the Yorkshire pudding in a little gravy to soften the edges.

Dinner

10-MINUTE PEA PASTA

This smooth and silky pasta is loaded with sweet, nutrient-dense peas, which results in a glorious pale green coloured sauce. If you don't own a stick blender, you can cook the peas in with the pasta by adding them to the water for the last 5 minutes of cooking and keep whole for a variation in texture, which is suitable from 6 months.

🍴 2 adults and 2 littles
or 1 adult and 1 little
with plenty of
leftovers for
tomorrow's pasta
bake (see page 38)

⏱ 10–12 minutes

250g (9oz) dried pasta
(gluten-free, if
required*)
200g (7oz) frozen peas
1 large garlic clove, sliced
400ml (14fl oz) full-fat
(whole) milk or
plant-based
alternative*
1 low-salt vegetable or
chicken stock cube
½ tsp dried mixed herbs
1 tbsp unsalted butter,
dairy-free spread or
coconut oil*
2 tbsp cornflour
(cornstarch)
100g (3½oz) Cheddar
cheese, grated (or
dairy-free grated
cheese, or 2 tbsp
nutritional yeast*)
freshly ground black
pepper

Fill a kettle to the top and set to boil. Meanwhile add 1cm (½in) depth of water to a large saucepan and set over a high heat. Once the kettle is boiled, the pan should be scorching hot. Add the boiled water and bring to a rolling boil – this should happen quickly, within a minute. Add the dried pasta and cook according to the packet instructions.

Add the frozen peas, sliced garlic and milk to a microwaveable jug. Cook in the microwave on high for 4 minutes until the milk is slightly warmed and the peas are no longer frozen.

Crumble the stock cube into the jug and add the mixed dried herbs, then whizz until smooth using a stick blender.

In a large non-stick frying pan set over a medium heat, melt the butter, then add the cornflour, whisking for a minute or so to remove the raw flour taste.

Gradually add the pea mixture, whisking continuously to remove any lumps. Keep whisking over the heat until the sauce has thickened, then turn the heat off and add the cheese and a good grinding of black pepper. Stir to melt the cheese into the sauce and set aside until the pasta is cooked.

Drain the cooked pasta and add it to the sauce, stir and serve. Babies can eat this dish as finger food if you use a nice long pasta shape like rigatoni or fusilli. Alternatively, you can blend baby's portion and serve on a spoon.

TRANSFORM YOUR LEFTOVERS!
Leftovers will keep for 2 days in the fridge, or head to page 38 to turn them into a delicious pasta bake with lots of extra goodness.

Or get ahead! The sauce can be frozen separately for up to 3 months; defrost, heat until piping hot and stir through freshly-cooked pasta for dinner in a hurry!

EASY BUTTERNUT SQUASH RISOTTO

With little ones to tend to, traditional risotto recipes aren't ideal in moments when baby suddenly starts to cry or kiddo needs help with their homework. Try this easy butternut squash risotto, ready in under 30 minutes with minimal "standing and stirring". It's utterly delicious too!

🍴 2 adults and 2 littles

⏱ 30 minutes

600g (1lb 5oz) butternut squash, peeled and cubed

1 tbsp garlic-infused olive oil

1 tsp sunflower oil

30g (1oz) unsalted butter or dairy-free alternative*

1 small brown onion, coarsely grated

2 garlic cloves, grated

250g (9oz) arborio risotto rice

1 low-salt vegetable or chicken stock cube

½ tsp ground cinnamon

70g (2½oz) Cheddar cheese, grated, or 2 tbsp nutritional yeast*

freshly ground black pepper

Preheat the oven to 220°C fan (240°C/475°F/Gas 9). Spread two-thirds of the squash out on a lined baking tray, drizzle with the garlic-infused oil and bake in the oven for 20 minutes.

Set a large sauté pan over medium heat and add the sunflower oil and half the butter to melt. Add the onion and garlic and fry, stirring continuously to avoid burning. After a minute or so, when the onions are becoming translucent, add the risotto rice and cook for a couple of minutes so the grains take on a little brown colour.

Meanwhile, measure 800ml (28fl oz) boiling water into a jug and crumble in the stock cube. Add a quarter of the stock to the rice, stirring well. Add the remaining squash cubes, along with a good grinding of black pepper and the ground cinnamon, and cook for a minute. Most of the stock should quickly be absorbed, then add the remaining liquid. Stir well and let the risotto bubble away on a medium–high heat. Keep an eye on it, stirring a little every 5 minutes or so. It should take 20–25 minutes to cook. If the water is evaporating quickly, add a good splash of water occasionally, but be careful to not add too much towards the end of the cooking. After 20 minutes, taste a few grains of rice and if they feel cooked with a slight firmness, the risotto is ready.

While the rice bubbles away, keep an eye on the squash in the oven. Once it's got some lovely charred edges, and the insides are soft, it's ready. Remove from the oven and set aside.

When the rice is cooked, roughly mash the chunks of squash in the risotto with a wooden spoon. Add the the grated cheese and remaining butter. Stir well and suddenly the risotto will become silky. Add half of the oven-roasted squash to the risotto and stir before serving with the remaining roasted squash as a garnish on each bowl. Adults, you may want to season your plate at the table with a little salt.

For baby's portion you can serve this risotto as it is, mashing large chunks of squash, or you can pop it in a blender and blitz.

LEFTOVER RISOTTO?
Cool it down and chill right away. When reheating, ensure the dish is piping hot all the way through. Try making a batch of What Mummy Makes arancini balls with the leftovers.

CREAMY PAPRIKA CHICKEN WITH SPINACH

EF

DF*

Soft and succulent chicken, coated in an irresistibly smooth paprika sauce, with added spinach for goodness. Serve with mashed potatoes and veg for a comforting meal the whole family will love.

🍴 2 adults and 2 littles

⏱ 20 minutes

1 tbsp garlic-infused olive oil

600g (1lb 5oz) mini chicken breast fillets (or 3 large chicken breasts, cut into chunky finger strips)

1 low-salt chicken stock cube

1 tsp dried mixed herbs

140ml (4¾fl oz) full-fat (whole) milk or plant-based alternative*

15g (½oz) unsalted butter or more garlic-infused olive oil*

1 heaped tsp cornflour (cornstarch)

2 heaped tsp smoked paprika

2 large garlic cloves, crushed

3 handfuls of baby leaf spinach

freshly ground black pepper

mashed potato, to serve

Put the oil in a large non-stick frying pan over a high heat. Add the chicken and fry for 8–10 minutes.

Meanwhile, crumble the stock cube into a jug, add the dried herbs, and cover with 160ml (5¼fl oz) hot boiled water. Stir to dissolve the stock cube, then add the milk and set aside.

Once the chicken is cooked all the way through and is a lovely brown colour on the outside, transfer it to a plate and set aside.

While the pan is still hot, but off the heat, melt the butter and add the cornflour, paprika and garlic. Stir well and cook for 30 seconds using the residual heat in the pan. Pop the pan back on the heat and gradually add the stock mixture, whisking continuously until the sauce has thickened.

Add the chicken back into the pan, including any resting juices, plus three handfuls of baby leaf spinach. Stir to coat the chicken and veggies in the sauce, helping the spinach to wilt.

Serve with a good helping of mash to soak up all of that delicious sauce. For baby's portion, cut the chicken in half lengthways so you have a thinner finger strip, which is easier for baby to hold. Serve the mash and sauce preloaded on a few spoons on rotation, or let baby embrace the mess and eat it with their hands.

Store the paprika chicken in an airtight container in the fridge for 2 days or for up to 3 months in the freezer.

REINVENT YOUR LEFTOVERS!

If you have any leftovers, how about making a few hand pies? Cut a sheet of puff pastry into 4 squares. Chop the chicken into chunks, and dollop 2 spoonfuls into the centre of each piece of pastry, along with a good coating of leftover sauce. Egg wash the edges, fold over and seal the pastry together. Brush the tops with more egg wash before baking at 200°C fan (220°C/425°F/Gas 7) for 15–20 minutes until puffed up and golden.

TOP TIP
Spread out a
spoonful or two on a
cold ceramic plate to cool
down for baby before you
dish out your own
portions.

30-MINUTE BABY-FRIENDLY LASAGNE

Whip up this delicious hidden-veg, lasagne-style bake in just 30 minutes. Swapping the traditional lasagne sheets for pasta shapes, which are easier for baby to hold, makes this dish suitable for the whole family. Serve with boiled veg or a salad.

🍴 2 adults and 2 littles
   with leftovers
⏱ 30 minutes

1 white onion
1 large courgette
   (zucchini)
200g (7oz) dried pasta,
   such as fusilli spirals
500g (1lb 2oz) lean
   minced (ground) beef
   (or plant-based
   alternative*)
1 low-salt beef stock cube
2 tsp dried mixed herbs
2 garlic cloves, crushed
1 heaped tsp smoked
   paprika
1 tbsp Worcestershire
   sauce (optional*)
500g (1lb 2oz) tomato
   passata
250g (9oz) ricotta
1 medium egg or 1 chia
   egg (see page 28)*
100g (3½oz) Cheddar
   cheese, grated
freshly ground black
   pepper

Preheat the oven to 220°C fan (240°C/475°F/Gas 8) and set a large sauté pan over a medium–high heat. Bring a separate saucepan of water to the boil, using a kettle to speed up the process.

Chop the onion in half and remove the brown skin. Then, coarsely grate the onion using a box grater. Grate the courgette too, discarding the end.

Roughly squeeze out a little of the juice from the onion and courgette and put them in the now-hot frying pan. Spread the mixture out in the pan so that most of the veg meets the hot surface and begin to cook quickly.

Add the pasta to the pan of boiling water and cook for 10 minutes, or according to the packet instructions.

Now, back to the veg pan: Once the onion and courgette have softened a little, add the beef and break it up using a wooden spoon. Cook for 5 minutes, stirring often, until the mince has browned throughout. Crumble in the stock cube and add the herbs, garlic, paprika, Worcestershire sauce and a good grinding of black pepper. Stir, then add the passata and give it all a good mix. Cook for a further couple of minutes, until the pasta is ready.

Meanwhile, prep the cheat's white sauce by mixing the ricotta, egg and half of the grated cheese in a bowl. Add a touch of ground black pepper too.

Drain the pasta and add it to the beef sauce. Transfer the whole lot to an ovenproof dish, large enough for the pasta to fit snuggly inside, then top with the white sauce. Spread the mixture evenly over the pasta and sprinkle the top with the remaining cheese.

Pop the dish in the hot oven to cook for 12–15 minutes, or until the cheese has melted and is starting to turn golden on top.Remove from the oven and allow to stand for a minute before serving.

FRIDAY FISH TACOS WITH HERBY COUSCOUS

Enjoy a family Mexican night with these impressively tasty fish tacos, served with a yogurt dip, pickled cucumber salad and herby couscous.

🍴 2 adults and 2 littles

⏱ 20 minutes

600g (1lb 5oz) skinless and boneless white flaky fish fillets, such as cod or basa
1 tsp smoked paprika
½ tsp ground cumin
juice of ½ lemon
1 tbsp low-salt soy sauce
1 tbsp garlic-infused olive oil
freshly ground black pepper
6 mini tortilla wraps

HERBY COUSCOUS
250g (9oz) couscous
1 low-salt chicken or vegetable stock cube
handful of parsley, finely chopped
juice of ½ lemon

PICKLED CUCUMBER SALAD
1 large cucumber
juice of ½ lemon
½ tsp sugar (optional)
2 tsp white wine vinegar

YOGURT DIP
4 tbsp Greek-style yogurt
juice of ½ lemon
1 tsp crushed garlic
pinch of smoked paprika

Preheat the oven to 200ºC fan (220ºC/425ºF/Gas 7).

Put the couscous in a bowl, crumble in the stock cube and rub the stock into the grains a little. Cover the couscous with boiling water, plus an extra 1cm (½in), stir, cover and set aside.

Lay the fish on a lined baking tray and add the paprika, cumin, lemon juice, soy sauce, olive oil and black pepper. Using your hands, spread the flavourings all over the fish. Pop in the oven for 10–12 minutes until the fish is firm and flakes easily.

Meanwhile, make the cucumber salad. Cut the cucumber into 7.5cm (3in) lengths, then slice each section into 5mm (¼in) slices. Gather together and cut into 5mm (¼in) thick matchsticks. Repeat with the remaining cucumber. Add to a bowl along with the lemon juice, sugar (if using) and vinegar, stir and set aside.

Set a griddle pan over a high heat while you make the yogurt dip. Combine all the dip ingredients in a small bowl and set aside.

One at a time, place a tortilla wrap on the searingly hot griddle pan for 30 seconds on each side until you see some char marks, then transfer onto a serving plate and repeat. You can skip this step but it really adds lots of flavour to the finished taco.

Remove the fish from the oven once cooked and set aside to rest.

Back to the couscous: Add the lemon juice, chopped parsley and a grinding of black pepper and give it a good mix.

Drain the cucumber salad and squeeze the cucumber a little to remove excess liquid – this stops your tacos getting soggy.

To assemble, add 1 tsp of yogurt dip to the centre of a tortilla wrap. Flake the fish into 2.5cm (1in) shards and layer a couple of pieces onto the taco. Top with 1 tbsp of the cucumber salad and a touch more yogurt dip. Pick up and dig in, accompanied by the couscous.

Serve each element deconstructed for baby, and cut half a tortilla wrap into finger strips to dunk into the yogurt dip.

SPICY BEAN BURGERS WITH OVEN CHIPS

Up your burger-night game with these protein-packed bean patties!

🍴 4 burgers, with
   2 extra burgers
   for the freezer

⏲ 30 minutes

600g (1lb 5oz) floury
   white potatoes, such
   as Maris Piper, washed
   and dried
400g (14oz) can
   cannellini beans,
   drained and rinsed
400g (14oz) can black
   beans, drained and
   rinsed
2 tsp smoked paprika
2 tsp ground cumin
2 tsp ground coriander
1 tsp garam masala
2 tsp crushed garlic
1 medium egg or 1 chia
   egg* (see page 28)
5 tbsp breadcrumbs
60g (2oz) Cheddar
   cheese, grated
1½ tbsp garlic-infused
   olive oil, plus a drizzle
   for the burgers

TO SERVE
Greek-style yogurt
1 garlic clove
2 gherkins, finely diced
1 avocado
squeeze of lemon juice
4 burger buns, halved
freshly ground black
   pepper

Preheat the oven to 220°C fan (240°C/475°F/Gas 9).

Slice the potatoes into 1cm (½in) thick chips (fries) and put in a glass bowl. Cover and microwave for 3 minutes on high.

Meanwhile, put the beans in a large bowl and mash well with a potato masher. Add the spices, garlic, egg, breadcrumbs and cheese and mix well. Divide the mixture into 6 portions and form each into a neat round patty. Place on a baking tray lined with non-stick baking paper and drizzle a little oil over each patty.

Transfer the chips to a large baking tray and spread into a thin even layer. Drizzle over the 1½ tbsp oil and stir to coat.

Place both trays in the oven, with the chips on the top shelf so that they will crisp up.

While everything bakes, prepare the accompaniments. Put the yogurt into a small bowl, finely grate or crush the garlic clove and add it to the bowl along with a small pinch of black pepper and the diced gherkin. Stir and set aside.

Peel and pit the avocado and cut into thin slices. Drizzle with a little lemon juice, as this stops the avocado browning too quickly.

In a hot frying pan, toast the cut-side of each brioche bun so it crisps up a little, adding flavour. (This is an optional step, if little ones are distracting you.)

After 15–20 minutes, the burger patties should be slightly crispy on the outside and firm to touch, but still soft in the middle. Remove the burgers from the oven. While the door is open, give the chips a little shake, then let them crisp up for a further 2 minutes.

Assemble the burgers by spreading a little of the yogurt dip on the base of the bun, top with a bean burger, some sliced avocado and a touch more yogurt dip, followed by the bun top. Serve with the chips on the side.

For little taste testers, serve the burgers deconstructed and cut into finger strips.

MINI EGGY-BREAD BROCCOLI QUICHES

These light and fluffy eggy cups with a little bonus broccoli are perfect after a heavy Sunday roast, but are also delicious for lunch at home or on the go. Serve with a picky salad and yogurt for dipping.

🍴 6 quiches
⏲ 25 minutes

butter or oil*, for
    greasing
½ head of broccoli
5 medium eggs
45g (1½oz) Cheddar
    cheese (optional*)
80ml (3fl oz) full-fat
    (whole) milk or
    plant-based
    alternative*
6 medium slices of white
    bread or gluten-free
    bread*
freshly ground black
    pepper

Preheat the oven to 200°C fan (220°C/425°F/Gas 7) and grease 6 holes in a non-stick muffin tray.

Using a box grater, coarsely grate the broccoli, discarding the woody stem. Transfer to a microwaveable bowl, cover and cook on high for 2 minutes.

Once the broccoli is part-cooked, put it in a mixing bowl with the eggs, cheese, milk and a good grinding of black pepper and whisk until well combined.

Cut the crusts off the bread and discard. Dip each piece of bread briefly into the egg mixture to soak, then press it into a hole in the muffin pan. Ensure the bread reaches the bottom corners and there is space in the middle for more filling to sit. Use your fingers to press the bread into a rough muffin case shape.

Spoon the remaining egg mixture between the bread cups, filling right to the top.

Bake the quiches for 15–20 minutes, or until the egg has puffed up and the bread has turned a little golden on the edges.

Allow to sit for a minute before running a knife around the edges and removing each quiche gently from the tray.

Any leftovers will keep in an airtight container in the fridge for 2 days.

BE FREEZER STASH SAVVY
These mini quiches freeze really well for up to 3 months. Defrost throughly, then reheat in a hot oven for 10 minutes or until piping hot throughout.

Snacks
and Puds

LEFTOVER PORRIDGE BLUEBERRY BARS

A little porridge from breakfast left in the pot? Don't throw it out: turn it into delicious blueberry oat bars.

🍴 12 bars
⏱ 25 minutes

2 medium bananas
200g (7oz) cold leftover porridge
250g (9oz) rolled (old-fashioned) porridge oats*
1 heaped tsp ground cinnamon
1 tbsp honey, or maple syrup if your little one is under 12 months old* (optional)
40ml (1¼fl oz) full-fat (whole) milk or plant-based alternative*
100g (3½oz) seedless raisins
50g (1¾oz) chopped or ground nuts
100g (3½oz) fresh blueberries

Preheat the oven to 200°C fan (220°C/425°F/Gas 7) and line a 20cm (8in) square baking pan with baking paper.

Mash the bananas in a mixing bowl with the back of a fork, then add all the remaining ingredients apart from the blueberries. Give it a good stir, then tip the mixture into the baking pan.

Using the back of a tablespoon, spread the mixture out evenly and press down to compact it, ensuring that the sides are pressed down well, too.

Tip the fresh blueberries on top and spread out evenly, then press the berries into the oats a little with the palm of your hand.

Pop in the oven and bake for 15–20 minutes, or until it feels firm to the touch and the edges are starting to brown.

Lift out the entire bake using the baking paper as handles and transfer to a chopping board. Cut into 12 long bars and allow to cool a little before digging in.

These blueberry bars will keep in an airtight container at room temperature for 4 days, or freeze for up to 3 months.

NO LEFTOVER PORRIDGE?
No problem! Add in an extra 100g (3½oz) oats and 80ml (2½fl oz) milk to replace the cold porridge.

NOTE
If using plant-based alternatives, choose a dairy-free cheese that melts well, as this will have the best outcome.

GARLIC AND POPPY SEED CRACKERS

Start the week by whipping up a batch of these savoury, melt in the mouth crackers, perfect for quick-grab snacks, an accompaniment to a picky plate or lunchboxes on the go. They're also the perfect vehicle to dunk in your favourite dip.

🍴 about 45 crackers

⏱ 20 minutes

85g (3oz) cold unsalted butter, cubed, or firm plant-based spread*

150g (5½oz) plain (all-purpose) flour

100g (3½oz) Cheddar cheese or plant-based Cheddar-style cheese*, grated

2 tsp garlic granules

2 heaped tbsp poppy seeds

1 small egg or 1 chia egg (see page 28)*

Preheat the oven to 200°C fan (220°C/425°F/Gas 7).

Put the butter and flour in a food processor and whizz briefly until it resembles fine breadcrumbs.

Now add the cheese, garlic and poppy seeds and whizz again.

Whisk the egg in a small bowl and gradually add to the food processor while blending on medium speed. Once the dough starts to clump together and clean the sides of the mixer, stop whizzing and tip it out onto a floured work surface.

Bring the dough together with your hands, then cut the dough in half. Roll out each portion to about 3mm (⅛in) thick, dusting with flour as you go. Keep moving the dough between each roll to ensure you get an even thickness and to stop it from sticking to the surface.

Trim the edges with a knife so that you have a clean cut rectangle or square, then cut into 7.5cm (3in) rectangle shapes. (You could also use a cookie cutter here to make the crackers any shape you like.) Transfer the crackers to a non-stick baking sheet, then gather up the excess dough, re-roll and repeat.

Bake the crackers for 8–10 minutes until coloured slightly and crisped up. Check them after 8 minutes as they can catch quickly. Once baked, transfer the crackers to a wire rack to cool.

The crackers will last in an airtight container for up to 1 week. You can also freeze some of the unbaked dough for another day; thaw completely before rolling out and cutting.

SUNSHINE PEACH MUFFINS

Bring a little summer to your kitchen with these colourful sweet peach muffins.

🍴 12 muffins

⏱ 25 minutes

2 x 410g (14oz) cans
peach slices or halves
in juice, drained
(500g/1lb 2oz total
drained weight)

160g (5¾oz) unsalted
butter, dairy-free
spread or coconut oil*,
melted, plus extra for
greasing

250g (9oz) self-raising
flour

1 tsp baking powder

60g (2oz) golden caster
sugar (optional)

3 medium eggs

2 tsp pure vanilla extract

2 tsp almond extract

Preheat the oven to 180°C fan (200°C/400°F/Gas 6) and grease a 12-hole non-stick muffin tray, or line with non-stick paper cases.

Add 250g (9oz) of the drained peaches to a mixing bowl and mash with a potato masher until every segment of peach has broken down. You don't need a smooth purée – a few small lumps are fine.

Add the melted butter, flour, baking powder, sugar (if using), eggs, and vanilla and almond extracts. Mix to combine, but be careful to avoid overworking the batter.

Divide the batter evenly between the 12 muffin holes.

Take the remaining peaches and slice into thin slivers. Decorate the tops of each muffin with a few slices of peach before popping in the oven. Bake for 20 minutes, or until an inserted sharp knife comes out clean.

The muffins will keep in airtight container at room temperature for 3–4 days, or in the freezer for up to 3 months.

TIP
You can swap out the peaches for pretty much any other canned fruit. Pears or pineapple would be delicious, just ensure it's in fruit juice rather than sugar syrup.

QUICK-GRAB SNACKS

Sometimes you really need to be able to pop in the kitchen for 60 seconds and pull out a tasty and nutritious snack that everyone will be happy with.

🍴 Serves the whole family
⏱ Less than 5 minutes

60-SECOND QUICK-GRAB IDEAS

- Avocado slices dipped in poppy or sesame seeds.

- Hard-boiled eggs* and cold cooked peas sprinkled with sesame seeds.

- Cheese* and crackers*.

- Thinly sliced apple and nut butter.

- Strawberries and thick Greek-style yogurt*.

- Sliced pears and Cheddar cheese* (grated or sliced).

- Frozen fruit yogurt: Whizz up your favourite fruit in a blender or mash with a fork. Mix through yogurt* and serve as is, or pop into ice lolly moulds for the easiest and healthiest ice lolly there is!

- Leftover cooked cold pasta* to mix with your favourite dip.

- Rice cakes topped with soft cream cheese* and chives or mashed banana.

- Strawberries and dry cereal*.

SNACKS THAT TAKE JUST A COUPLE OF MINUTES TO WHIP UP

- Peanut butter and banana bites: Thickly slice bananas, then sandwich two discs together with a generous smear of 100% peanut butter. You can coat them in melted chocolate* for an extra-special treat, and even freeze them to pull out on warm summer days.

- Banana sushi: Coat a peeled banana in Greek-style yogurt*, peanut butter or cream cheese*, then roll in your choice of toppings. Crushed nuts, desiccated (dried shredded) coconut, pomegranate seeds and crushed cereals* all work well. For an extra-special treat, try chocolate spread* with crushed hazelnuts – it's a game changer!

- Tuna pâté: Drain a can of tuna in spring water* and mix with 3 tbsp Greek-style yogurt*, a little lemon juice and freshly ground black pepper. The perfect dip for crackers, toast or veggie sticks.

- Raspberries mashed with the back of a fork and spread on toast fingers.

- Grated ripe plum flesh mixed with cottage cheese* and a little ground cinnamon.

- A quick fridge/freezer-raid smoothie with fresh or frozen fruit and veg.

- Mashed avocado with lemon juice, a little Greek-style yogurt*, ½ tsp of garlic granules and a touch of freshly ground black pepper.

- Bean dip: Drain 1 can of cannellini beans and blend with 100ml (3½fl oz) of sour cream*, ½ crushed garlic clove and a small bunch of chives. Add a little black pepper for seasoning. Perfect paired with crackers*.

PB, CHOC AND STRAWBERRY FRO-YO SLICE

A moreish peanut butter and chocolate flavoured oat base, topped with a refreshing strawberry frozen yogurt. When I served this one to my Nina, she devoured the whole thing in 5 minutes and proceeded to ask for more. I just know I was onto a winner!

🍴 8 slices

⏱ 20 minutes, plus freezing time

200g (7oz) fresh strawberries, hulled and halved, plus extra for decoration

300g (10½oz) Greek-style yogurt or plant-based alternative*

100g (3½oz) rolled (old-fashioned) porridge oats*

1½ tbsp honey, or maple syrup if your little one is under 12 months old* (optional)

60g (2oz) smooth or crunchy 100% peanut butter

1 tbsp unsweetened cocoa powder

small handful of flaked (slivered) almonds or crushed nuts

small handful of chocolate chips (optional)

Take a 900g (2lb) loaf tin and cut a strip of baking paper to the same length as the pan and up the sides. Line the base – this helps you remove the fro-yo slice once it's frozen solid.

Put the strawberries into a flat-bottomed bowl and mash them with a fork or potato masher. Add the yogurt, mix and set aside.

To make the oat base, put the porridge oats in a mixing bowl, along with the honey, peanut butter, cocoa powder and 3 tbsp of the yogurt mixture. Mix well to ensure it's all fully combined.

Now, to assemble, spoon the oat mixture into the base of the tin, spread out evenly, then press it down with the back of a spoon, ensuring the edges aren't raised and the top is as level as you can get it.

Top with the remaining yogurt mixture and spread evenly. Decorate the top with thinly sliced strawberries and flaked almonds. You could even add some choc chips if you fancy! Cover and freeze for at least 4 hours or until solid throughout.

Once set, remove from the freezer and lift the entire block from the tin and place on a chopping board. Allow to thaw for at least 10–20 minutes.

Now the fro-yo bars have softened ever so slightly, use a large sharp knife, with your free hand on top of the blade (keeping your fingers spread out) to firmly slice the block widthways into bars around 2cm (¾in) wide. You can enjoy straight away or pop back in the freezer to enjoy another day. Store in a freezer bag or container.

These yummy frozen bars will last for 3 months in the freezer.

GARLIC DOUGH BALLS

Soft and yummy bread buns, coated in a delicious garlic butter. Paired with your favourite pasta dish or enjoyed on their own, they really won't stick around long!

🍴 2 adults and 2 littles

⏱ 25 minutes

250g (9oz) self-raising flour, plus extra for dusting
250g (9oz) Greek-style yogurt or plant-based alternative*
100g (3½oz) Cheddar cheese, grated, or 2 tbsp nutritional yeast*
1 tsp baking powder
1 tsp garlic granules
freshly ground black pepper

GARLIC BUTTER

50g (1¾oz) unsalted butter or dairy-free spread*, plus extra for greasing
2 large garlic cloves, finely crushed
1 tbsp finely chopped parsley

Preheat the oven to 200°C fan (220°C/425°F/Gas 7) and grease a 20cm (8in) round baking dish, or similar shape and size, with butter.

Put the flour, yogurt, cheese, baking powder, garlic granules and a little freshly ground black pepper into a bowl and mix until it starts to clump together.

Tip out onto a floured work surface and knead the dough together in your hands until it forms a ball. Dust with extra flour if you feel it's too sticky. Using a sharp knife, cut the dough into 8 portions. Tip a small pile of flour onto the work surface, then one at a time, take a piece of dough and briefly roll the sticky cut edges in the flour. Roll the dough between your hands to form a neat ball, place in the baking dish and repeat with the rest of the dough until you have 8 balls of dough sitting snuggly in the dish.

Pop in the oven to bake for 15 minutes, or until puffed up and the tops have turned a golden-brown colour.

While the dough balls bake, prepare the garlic butter by adding the butter and crushed garlic to a small pan and melting completely. Add the chopped parsley and a good grinding of black pepper and set aside until the dough balls are baked.

Once the dough balls feel springy to the touch, and when tapped carefully with your finger they sound hollow, remove from the oven. Immediately brush over the garlic butter using a pastry brush, ensuring you coat the entire surface with a little butter.

Allow to sit for a minute to soak before digging in.

BERRY BREAD AND BUTTER PUDDING

Soft on the inside, and irresistibly crispy on top! Serve with custard or yogurt for a healthier take on a much-loved British classic. You could even enjoy it for breakfast, if you wish!

🍴 4 adults and 2 littles

⏱ 30 minutes

280ml (9½fl oz) full-fat (whole) milk or plant-based alternative*

2 tsp pure vanilla extract

150ml (5fl oz) double (heavy) cream or plant-based alternative*

butter, sunflower or coconut oil, for greasing

4 thick slices of white bread

4 stale croissants (or double up on bread*)

100g (3½oz) mixed berries (blueberries, raspberries, blackberries)

4 medium eggs, beaten

1 tbsp demerara (turbinado) sugar (optional)

Preheat the oven to 180°C fan (200°C/400°F/Gas 6).

Put the milk, vanilla and cream in a saucepan and warm over a medium–high heat until scolding but not boiling.

Meanwhile, grease a 1.3 litre (1¼ quart) ovenproof dish.

Very roughly break up the bread and croissants into chunks, placing in the dish. Add the berries and mix so that the fruit is evenly slotted between the bread pieces.

Once the milk and cream mixture is hot, remove from the heat and add the eggs, quickly whisking to avoid the eggs scrambling.

Pour the runny custard evenly over the bread and berries, then, with the back of spoon, gently press any pieces of bread that are sticking out of the custard down into the liquid to soak. Allow to stand for a minute while you add a sprinkle of sugar to the top (if using). Pop the dish in the oven and bake for 20–25 minutes, until golden on top and risen well.

Spoon into chunks and allow to cool before letting baby dig in with their hands.

Leftovers will keep for a couple of days, covered, in the fridge. Reheat in a hot oven for 10 minutes until piping hot throughout.

CHOCCY TWIST
If you have a sweet tooth, dot 100g (3½oz) chocolate chunks into the pudding before baking for a scrumptious treat for older children.

Meal Planning

How to use your family meal planner

Take the stress out of the dinner rush: no more 4pm cupboard raid while your kids shout that they're "hunnngrrry", and say goodbye to the aimless "what shall I cook today?" supermarket wonder. Instead, spend just 30 minutes each week planning the meals for your week ahead and organise the food shop so you have everything needed to quickly whip up your family's favourite feasts.

Starting with a blank weekly meal plan, what's the first thing to do?

1. Check what you have in the fridge already that needs using up. Do you have any veg that's turning or meat that's about to go off? Write down what these are in the "What have we got in?" box.

2. Starting with the ingredients that need using up, think of a couple of meals which require these ingredients for the start of the week. Use the index in the What Mummy Makes cookbook to help find recipes using certain ingredients.

3. Fill up the rest of the week with meals you fancy cooking and eating that week – there's no point in filling the meal plan with recipes you're not that fussed about. You have to want to eat the food in the plan, otherwise your planning will quickly go out the window.

4. Once you have completed your weekly meal plan, write up your shopping list so you don't forget anything. Remember to buy things to go on the side too, always thinking about the make up of your perfect plate, see page 9!

5. If you have time, once you have all of your food shopping, prep some of the veggies by washing them and storing in reusable bags or containers in the fridge. But don't worry if the day runs away with you – this isn't a necessity.

6. If you've made a meal that your family loved, jot it down in the list of family favourites on page 16, to refer back to when planning future weekly menus.

TIPS FOR EFFICIENT MEAL PLANNING

Meal planning can seem daunting when you first start doing it. If you feel overwhelmed, use your meal plan as a rough guide to what you plan to eat that week, but don't worry about sticking to it completely. Change up days

here and there depending on what you fancy eating that day; it's your plan, there are no strict rules!

- Don't worry about your plan running from Monday to Sunday – if Monday meal planning and shopping doesn't work for you, then start the week on any day you like.

- Plan for meals off, so you don't feel so overwhelmed, plus, who has the time to be cooking four times a day all week long? Try to account for using up leftovers or eating out.

- Make a big batch of lunch or dinner recipes so you have plenty for the next day.

- Utilise your freezer: stock up on frozen veggies for quick-grab sides and cook extra portions so you can take days off from cooking.

- When writing your meal plan, think about the main element to the meal, for example fritters, but also plan what you will have on the side like cucumber and yogurt so this gets added to the shopping list too.

Example

Weekly Meal Planner

Date 10 December

#WMMEALPLANNING

WHAT NEEDS USING UP

Creamy paprika chicken with mash and veg (leftovers make a great pie)
Half a cucumber
A little Greek-style yogurt

Leftover chicken from the Sunday roast

NOTES - EVENTS TO REMEMBER

Parents' evening on Wednesday
Grandma coming round for lunch on Sunday

	BREAKFAST	LUNCH	DINNER	SNACKS AND PUDS
MONDAY	Plentiful porridge	Spiced carrot sheet-pan fritters	10-minute pea pasta	Leftover porridge blueberry bars
TUESDAY	Sweet breakfast pinwheels	Salmon and broccoli pasta bake	Spiced carrot sheet-pan fritters, boiled eggs and salad	Garlic and poppy seed crackers
WEDNESDAY	Leftover porridge blueberry bars	Sweet breakfast pinwheels	Creamy paprika chicken with spinach	Pear slices and nut butter
THURSDAY	Cereal or toast	Leftover mashed potato cakes	30-minute baby-friendly lasagne	Sunshine peach muffins
FRIDAY	Sunshine peach muffins	30-minute baby-friendly lasagne	Friday fish tacos with herby couscous	PB, choc and strawberry fro-yo slice
SATURDAY	Blueberry breakfast cobbler	Pizza eggy bread roll-ups	Takeaway night!	Garlic and poppy seed crackers
SUNDAY	Dippy eggs with cheesy crumpet soldiers	30-minute Sunday roast	Mini eggy-bread broccoli quiche	Berry bread and butter pudding

Top tips for speedy shopping

With kids in tow, a lengthy leisurely shopping trip isn't always on the cards. Here are a few tips to make the process go a little more smoothly (and quickly!), meaning you're less likely to get home feeling stressed and to have forgotten what you went for in the first place!

- Check what's in the cupboards at home first to save any deliberating and filling up your kitchen with duplicates. This will save you money too!

- Categorise your shopping list in relation to where everything sits in the store.

- Take a snack for the kids to keep them entertained – something like a rice cake or an apple, which takes a little longer to get through than softer foods.

- If possible, try not to do a food shop when you are hungry: rumbling tummies always equal overspending!

- Head to the shops in off-peak times, avoiding the post-school run rush!

- Buy a few extra store pantry staples like pasta or tomato passata for quick off-plan meals that can be whipped up in no time.

- Grab fresh ingredients from the back of the shelf with a long sell-by date, these will keep for longer at home and help you to avoid wastage.

- Load up the checkout conveyor belt in categories, so when you're bagging your shopping out, it's all roughly in the right bags to unload quickly when you get home, too.

- And if you just don't have the time, an online grocery shop is always a good option!

Remember, when cooking for little ones, it's good to be mindful of the salt content of the foods you offer them. So take a quick glance at the nutritional information at the back of the product packaging, and do a rough little calculation of how much baby will actually be consuming in one sitting.

DON'T
FORGET TO PICK
SOMETHING UP
FOR YOU, MAMA

- you
deserve it!

Shopping List

CHILLED

500g lean minced beef ✓
250g ricotta
500g block Cheddar cheese
400g unsalted butter
4 pints whole milk
1kg chicken thighs
600g mini chicken breast fillets
    (or 3 large breasts)
2 x 500g tubs Greek-style yogurt
small pot of double cream
small pack of cream cheese
500–600g white flaky fish fillets,
    skinless and boneless (cod or
    basa)
2–3 skinless salmon fillets
1 sheet ready-rolled puff pastry

FRUIT & VEG

2 large courgettes
2 white onions
2 garlic bulbs
3 unwaxed lemons
1kg new potatoes
300g berries (mix of blueberries,
    raspberries, blackberries)
250g strawberries
big bunch of bananas
a handful of eating apples
bag of baby leaf spinach
2 broccoli heads
2 large cucumbers
bag of salad leaves
bunch of parsley
1kg carrots
bag of easy peel satsumas
punnet of kiwis

DATE 10 December

STORE CUPBOARD

- 450g dried pasta
- 500g tomato passata
- 2 dozen eggs
- 2 loaves of sliced bread
- small bag of ground almonds
- crumpets
- 4-8 croissants
- 6 mini tortilla wraps
- dried couscous
- bag of seedless raisins
- bag of chopped mixed nuts
- 2 cans of peach slices or halves
  (in juice)
- golden caster sugar

FROZEN

- bag of frozen peas
- 400g frozen blueberries
- ice cubes
- frozen garlic
- frozen herbs

EXTRAS

- washing up liquid
- cat food

£57.87

COST

Monthly kitchen inventory

I don't know about you, but I've been known to have rainy day cans and jars of spices that are way past their best lingering in my kitchen cupboards for far longer than I care to admit. Use this space to remind yourself to do a little check of what's in your cupboards once a month. Remove anything that is no longer edible and take note in next week's meal plan under "What needs using up?", so that it prompts you to reduce any future food waste in your kitchen.

	STORE CUPBOARD	BAKING AND SPICES	FRIDGE	FREEZER
MONTH:........ *January* DAY:*7th*	✔ 2x paprika *Example*	✔	✔	✔ low on peas
MONTH:........ .... DAY:..............				
MONTH:........ .... DAY:..............				
MONTH:........ .... DAY:..............				

	STORE CUPBOARD	BAKING AND SPICES	FRIDGE	FREEZER
MONTH:........ .... DAY:..............				
MONTH:........ .... DAY:..............				
MONTH:........ .... DAY:..............				
MONTH:........ .... DAY:..............				
MONTH:........ .... DAY:..............				
MONTH:........ .... DAY:..............				
MONTH:........ .... DAY:..............				
MONTH:........ .... DAY:..............				

Weekly Meal Planner

Date....................

WHAT NEEDS USING UP?

NOTES – EVENTS TO REMEMBER

	BREAKFAST	LUNCH	DINNER	SNACKS AND PUDS
MONDAY				
TUESDAY				
WEDNESDAY				
THURSDAY				
FRIDAY				
SATURDAY				
SUNDAY				

Shopping List

CHILLED

- ....
- ....
- ....
- ....
- ....
- ....
- ....
- ....
- ....
- ....
- ....
- ....
- ....
- ....
- ....
- ....
- ....
- ....
- ....
- ....
- ....
- ....

FRUIT & VEG

- ....
- ....
- ....
- ....
- ....
- ....
- ....
- ....
- ....
- ....
- ....
- ....
- ....
- ....
- ....
- ....
- ....
- ....
- ....
- ....
- ....
- ....

DATE ....

STORE CUPBOARD

FROZEN

EXTRAS

COST

Weekly Meal Planner

Date.....................

WHAT NEEDS USING UP?

....
....
....
....
....
....
....

NOTES – EVENTS TO REMEMBER

....
....
....
....
....
....

	BREAKFAST	LUNCH	DINNER	SNACKS AND PUDS
MONDAY				
TUESDAY				
WEDNESDAY				
THURSDAY				
FRIDAY				
SATURDAY				
SUNDAY				

Shopping List

CHILLED

- ....
- ....
- ....
- ....
- ....
- ....
- ....
- ....
- ....
- ....
- ....
- ....
- ....
- ....
- ....
- ....
- ....
- ....
- ....
- ....
- ....
- ....
- ....
- ....

FRUIT & VEG

- ....
- ....
- ....
- ....
- ....
- ....
- ....
- ....
- ....
- ....
- ....
- ....
- ....
- ....
- ....
- ....
- ....
- ....
- ....
- ....
- ....
- ....
- ....
- ....

DATE ....

STORE CUPBOARD

....

....

....

....

....

....

....

....

....

....

....

....

....

....

....

....

....

....

....

....

....

....

....

....

....

FROZEN

....

....

....

....

....

....

....

....

....

....

....

....

....

EXTRAS

....

....

....

....

....

....

....

....

....

.... COST

Weekly Meal Planner

Date....................

WHAT NEEDS USING UP?

....
....
....
....
....
....
....

NOTES – EVENTS TO REMEMBER

....
....
....
....
....
....

	BREAKFAST	LUNCH	DINNER	SNACKS AND PUDS
MONDAY				
TUESDAY				
WEDNESDAY				
THURSDAY				
FRIDAY				
SATURDAY				
SUNDAY				

Shopping List

CHILLED

FRUIT & VEG

DATE ....

STORE CUPBOARD

FROZEN

EXTRAS

COST

Weekly Meal Planner

Date.....................

WHAT NEEDS USING UP?

....
....
....
....
....
....
....

NOTES – EVENTS TO REMEMBER

....
....
....
....
....
....

	BREAKFAST	LUNCH	DINNER	SNACKS AND PUDS
MONDAY				
TUESDAY				
WEDNESDAY				
THURSDAY				
FRIDAY				
SATURDAY				
SUNDAY				

Shopping List

CHILLED

.... ●
.... ●
.... ●
.... ●
.... ●
.... ●
.... ●
.... ●
.... ●
.... ●
.... ●
.... ●
.... ●
.... ●
.... ●
.... ●
.... ●
.... ●
.... ●
.... ●
.... ●
.... ●
.... ●

FRUIT & VEG

.... ●
.... ●
.... ●
.... ●
.... ●
.... ●
.... ●
.... ●
.... ●
.... ●
.... ●
.... ●
.... ●
.... ●
.... ●
.... ●
.... ●
.... ●
.... ●
.... ●
.... ●
.... ●
.... ●

DATE ....

STORE CUPBOARD

- ....
- ....
- ....
- ....
- ....
- ....
- ....
- ....
- ....
- ....
- ....
- ....
- ....
- ....
- ....
- ....
- ....
- ....
- ....
- ....
- ....
- ....
- ....
- ....
- ....
- ....

FROZEN

- ....
- ....
- ....
- ....
- ....
- ....
- ....
- ....
- ....
- ....
- ....
- ....
- ....

EXTRAS

- ....
- ....
- ....
- ....
- ....
- ....
- ....
- ....
- ....
- ....

.... COST

Weekly Meal Planner

Date.....................

WHAT NEEDS USING UP?

....
....
....
....
....
....

NOTES – EVENTS TO REMEMBER

....
....
....
....
....
....

	BREAKFAST	LUNCH	DINNER	SNACKS AND PUDS
MONDAY				
TUESDAY				
WEDNESDAY				
THURSDAY				
FRIDAY				
SATURDAY				
SUNDAY				

Shopping List

CHILLED

....
....
....
....
....
....
....
....
....
....
....
....
....
....
....
....
....
....
....
....
....
....
....
....

FRUIT & VEG

....
....
....
....
....
....
....
....
....
....
....
....
....
....
....
....
....
....
....
....
....
....
....
....

DATE ....

STORE CUPBOARD

FROZEN

EXTRAS

COST

Weekly Meal Planner

Date.....................

WHAT NEEDS USING UP?

NOTES – EVENTS TO REMEMBER

	BREAKFAST	LUNCH	DINNER	SNACKS AND PUDS
MONDAY				
TUESDAY				
WEDNESDAY				
THURSDAY				
FRIDAY				
SATURDAY				
SUNDAY				

Shopping List

CHILLED

....
....
....
....
....
....
....
....
....
....
....
....
....
....
....
....
....
....
....
....
....
....

FRUIT & VEG

....
....
....
....
....
....
....
....
....
....
....
....
....
....
....
....
....
....
....
....
....
....

DATE ....

STORE CUPBOARD

- .... ●
- .... ●
- .... ●
- .... ●
- .... ●
- .... ●
- .... ●
- .... ●
- .... ●
- .... ●
- .... ●
- .... ●
- .... ●
- .... ●
- .... ●
- .... ●
- .... ●
- .... ●
- .... ●
- .... ●
- .... ●
- .... ●
- .... ●
- .... ●
- .... ●
- .... ●

FROZEN

- .... ●
- .... ●
- .... ●
- .... ●
- .... ●
- .... ●
- .... ●
- .... ●
- .... ●
- .... ●
- .... ●
- .... ●
- .... ●
- .... ●

EXTRAS

- .... ●
- .... ●
- .... ●
- .... ●
- .... ●
- .... ●
- .... ●
- .... ●
- .... ●

.... **COST**

You've got
THIS MAMAS!

Weekly Meal Planner

Date....................

WHAT NEEDS USING UP?

....
....
....
....
....
....
....

NOTES – EVENTS TO REMEMBER

....
....
....
....
....
....

	BREAKFAST	LUNCH	DINNER	SNACKS AND PUDS
MONDAY				
TUESDAY				
WEDNESDAY				
THURSDAY				
FRIDAY				
SATURDAY				
SUNDAY				

Shopping List

CHILLED

.... ●
.... ●
.... ●
.... ●
.... ●
.... ●
.... ●
.... ●
.... ●
.... ●
.... ●
.... ●
.... ●
.... ●
.... ●
.... ●
.... ●
.... ●
.... ●
.... ●
.... ●

FRUIT & VEG

.... ○
.... ○
.... ○
.... ○
.... ○
.... ○
.... ○
.... ○
.... ○
.... ○
.... ○
.... ○
.... ○
.... ○
.... ○
.... ○
.... ○
.... ○
.... ○
.... ○
.... ○

DATE ....

STORE CUPBOARD

.... ●
.... ●
.... ●
.... ●
.... ●
.... ●
.... ●
.... ●
.... ●
.... ●
.... ●
.... ●
.... ●
.... ●
.... ●
.... ●
.... ●
.... ●
.... ●
.... ●
.... ●
.... ●
.... ●
.... ●

FROZEN

.... ●
.... ●
.... ●
.... ●
.... ●
.... ●
.... ●
.... ●
.... ●
.... ●
.... ●
.... ●
.... ●
.... ●

EXTRAS

.... ●
.... ●
.... ●
.... ●
.... ●
.... ●
.... ●
.... ●
.... ●
.... ●

.... **COST**

Weekly Meal Planner

Date.........................

WHAT NEEDS USING UP?

....
....
....
....
....
....
....

NOTES – EVENTS TO REMEMBER

....
....
....
....
....
....

	BREAKFAST	LUNCH	DINNER	SNACKS AND PUDS
MONDAY				
TUESDAY				
WEDNESDAY				
THURSDAY				
FRIDAY				
SATURDAY				
SUNDAY				

Shopping List

CHILLED

- .... ●
- .... ●
- .... ●
- .... ●
- .... ●
- .... ●
- .... ●
- .... ●
- .... ●
- .... ●
- .... ●
- .... ●
- .... ●
- .... ●
- .... ●
- .... ●
- .... ●
- .... ●
- .... ●
- .... ●
- .... ●
- .... ●
- .... ●

FRUIT & VEG

- .... ●
- .... ●
- .... ●
- .... ●
- .... ●
- .... ●
- .... ●
- .... ●
- .... ●
- .... ●
- .... ●
- .... ●
- .... ●
- .... ●
- .... ●
- .... ●
- .... ●
- .... ●
- .... ●
- .... ●
- .... ●
- .... ●
- .... ●

DATE ....

STORE CUPBOARD

FROZEN

EXTRAS

COST

Weekly Meal Planner

Date.....................

WHAT NEEDS USING UP?

....
....
....
....
....
....
....

NOTES – EVENTS TO REMEMBER

....
....
....
....
....
....

	BREAKFAST	LUNCH	DINNER	SNACKS AND PUDS
MONDAY				
TUESDAY				
WEDNESDAY				
THURSDAY				
FRIDAY				
SATURDAY				
SUNDAY				

Shopping List

CHILLED

.... ●
.... ●
.... ●
.... ●
.... ●
.... ●
.... ●
.... ●
.... ●
.... ●
.... ●
.... ●
.... ●
.... ●
.... ●
.... ●
.... ●
.... ●
.... ●
.... ●
.... ●
.... ●
.... ●

FRUIT & VEG

.... ●
.... ●
.... ●
.... ●
.... ●
.... ●
.... ●
.... ●
.... ●
.... ●
.... ●
.... ●
.... ●
.... ●
.... ●
.... ●
.... ●
.... ●
.... ●
.... ●
.... ●
.... ●
.... ●

DATE ....

STORE CUPBOARD

FROZEN

EXTRAS

COST

Weekly Meal Planner

Date.....................

WHAT NEEDS USING UP?

....
....
....
....
....
....

NOTES – EVENTS TO REMEMBER

....
....
....
....
....
....

	BREAKFAST	LUNCH	DINNER	SNACKS AND PUDS
MONDAY				
TUESDAY				
WEDNESDAY				
THURSDAY				
FRIDAY				
SATURDAY				
SUNDAY				

Shopping List

CHILLED

- .... ○
- .... ○
- .... ○
- .... ○
- .... ○
- .... ○
- .... ○
- .... ○
- .... ○
- .... ○
- .... ○
- .... ○
- .... ○
- .... ○
- .... ○
- .... ○
- .... ○
- .... ○
- .... ○
- .... ○
- .... ○
- .... ○
- .... ○

FRUIT & VEG

- .... ○
- .... ○
- .... ○
- .... ○
- .... ○
- .... ○
- .... ○
- .... ○
- .... ○
- .... ○
- .... ○
- .... ○
- .... ○
- .... ○
- .... ○
- .... ○
- .... ○
- .... ○
- .... ○
- .... ○
- .... ○
- .... ○
- .... ○

DATE ....

STORE CUPBOARD

FROZEN

EXTRAS

COST

Weekly Meal Planner

Date.....................

WHAT NEEDS USING UP?

NOTES – EVENTS TO REMEMBER

	BREAKFAST	LUNCH	DINNER	SNACKS AND PUDS
MONDAY				
TUESDAY				
WEDNESDAY				
THURSDAY				
FRIDAY				
SATURDAY				
SUNDAY				

Shopping List

CHILLED

.... ⬤
.... ⬤
.... ⬤
.... ⬤
.... ⬤
.... ⬤
.... ⬤
.... ⬤
.... ⬤
.... ⬤
.... ⬤
.... ⬤
.... ⬤
.... ⬤
.... ⬤
.... ⬤
.... ⬤
.... ⬤
.... ⬤
.... ⬤
.... ⬤
.... ⬤
.... ⬤

FRUIT & VEG

.... ⬤
.... ⬤
.... ⬤
.... ⬤
.... ⬤
.... ⬤
.... ⬤
.... ⬤
.... ⬤
.... ⬤
.... ⬤
.... ⬤
.... ⬤
.... ⬤
.... ⬤
.... ⬤
.... ⬤
.... ⬤
.... ⬤
.... ⬤
.... ⬤
.... ⬤
.... ⬤

DATE ....

STORE CUPBOARD

FROZEN

EXTRAS

COST

Weekly Meal Planner

Date.....................

WHAT NEEDS USING UP?

....
....
....
....
....
....

NOTES – EVENTS TO REMEMBER

....
....
....
....
....
....

	BREAKFAST	LUNCH	DINNER	SNACKS AND PUDS
MONDAY				
TUESDAY				
WEDNESDAY				
THURSDAY				
FRIDAY				
SATURDAY				
SUNDAY				

Shopping List

CHILLED

.... ●
.... ●
.... ●
.... ●
.... ●
.... ●
.... ●
.... ●
.... ●
.... ●
.... ●
.... ●
.... ●
.... ●
.... ●
.... ●
.... ●
.... ●
.... ●
.... ●
.... ●
.... ●
.... ●

FRUIT & VEG

.... ●
.... ●
.... ●
.... ●
.... ●
.... ●
.... ●
.... ●
.... ●
.... ●
.... ●
.... ●
.... ●
.... ●
.... ●
.... ●
.... ●
.... ●
.... ●
.... ●
.... ●
.... ●

DATE ....

STORE CUPBOARD

FROZEN

EXTRAS

COST

PLANNING
TODAY

makes
tomorrow
a
DODDLE

Weekly Meal Planner

Date.....................

WHAT NEEDS USING UP?

....
....
....
....
....
....
....

NOTES – EVENTS TO REMEMBER

....
....
....
....
....
....

	BREAKFAST	LUNCH	DINNER	SNACKS AND PUDS
MONDAY				
TUESDAY				
WEDNESDAY				
THURSDAY				
FRIDAY				
SATURDAY				
SUNDAY				

Shopping List

CHILLED

.... ●
.... ●
.... ●
.... ●
.... ●
.... ●
.... ●
.... ●
.... ●
.... ●
.... ●
.... ●
.... ●
.... ●
.... ●
.... ●
.... ●
.... ●
.... ●
.... ●
.... ●
.... ●
.... ●
.... ●
.... ●

FRUIT & VEG

.... ●
.... ●
.... ●
.... ●
.... ●
.... ●
.... ●
.... ●
.... ●
.... ●
.... ●
.... ●
.... ●
.... ●
.... ●
.... ●
.... ●
.... ●
.... ●
.... ●
.... ●
.... ●
.... ●
.... ●
.... ●

DATE ....

STORE CUPBOARD

FROZEN

EXTRAS

Weekly Meal Planner

Date....................

WHAT NEEDS USING UP?

....
....
....
....
....
....
....

NOTES – EVENTS TO REMEMBER

....
....
....
....
....
....

	BREAKFAST	LUNCH	DINNER	SNACKS AND PUDS
MONDAY				
TUESDAY				
WEDNESDAY				
THURSDAY				
FRIDAY				
SATURDAY				
SUNDAY				

Shopping List

CHILLED

- ....
- ....
- ....
- ....
- ....
- ....
- ....
- ....
- ....
- ....
- ....
- ....
- ....
- ....
- ....
- ....
- ....
- ....
- ....
- ....
- ....
- ....

FRUIT & VEG

- ....
- ....
- ....
- ....
- ....
- ....
- ....
- ....
- ....
- ....
- ....
- ....
- ....
- ....
- ....
- ....
- ....
- ....
- ....
- ....
- ....
- ....

DATE ....

STORE CUPBOARD

FROZEN

EXTRAS

Weekly Meal Planner

Date....................

WHAT NEEDS USING UP?

....
....
....
....
....
....
....

NOTES – EVENTS TO REMEMBER

....
....
....
....
....
....

	BREAKFAST	LUNCH	DINNER	SNACKS AND PUDS
MONDAY				
TUESDAY				
WEDNESDAY				
THURSDAY				
FRIDAY				
SATURDAY				
SUNDAY				

Shopping List

CHILLED

FRUIT & VEG

STORE CUPBOARD

FROZEN

EXTRAS

COST

Weekly Meal Planner

Date....................

WHAT NEEDS USING UP?

....
....
....
....
....
....

NOTES – EVENTS TO REMEMBER

....
....
....
....
....
....

	BREAKFAST	LUNCH	DINNER	SNACKS AND PUDS
MONDAY				
TUESDAY				
WEDNESDAY				
THURSDAY				
FRIDAY				
SATURDAY				
SUNDAY				

Shopping List

CHILLED

....
....
....
....
....
....
....
....
....
....
....
....
....
....
....
....
....
....
....
....
....
....
....

FRUIT & VEG

....
....
....
....
....
....
....
....
....
....
....
....
....
....
....
....
....
....
....
....
....
....
....

DATE ....

STORE CUPBOARD

FROZEN

EXTRAS

COST

Weekly Meal Planner

Date...................

WHAT NEEDS USING UP?

NOTES – EVENTS TO REMEMBER

	BREAKFAST	LUNCH	DINNER	SNACKS AND PUDS
MONDAY				
TUESDAY				
WEDNESDAY				
THURSDAY				
FRIDAY				
SATURDAY				
SUNDAY				

Shopping List

CHILLED

....
....
....
....
....
....
....
....
....
....
....
....
....
....
....
....
....
....
....
....
....
....

FRUIT & VEG

....
....
....
....
....
....
....
....
....
....
....
....
....
....
....
....
....
....
....
....
....
....

DATE ....

STORE CUPBOARD

- .... ●
- .... ●
- .... ●
- .... ●
- .... ●
- .... ●
- .... ●
- .... ●
- .... ●
- .... ●
- .... ●
- .... ●
- .... ●
- .... ●
- .... ●
- .... ●
- .... ●
- .... ●
- .... ●
- .... ●
- .... ●
- .... ●
- .... ●
- .... ●
- .... ●

FROZEN

- .... ●
- .... ●
- .... ●
- .... ●
- .... ●
- .... ●
- .... ●
- .... ●
- .... ●
- .... ●
- .... ●
- .... ●
- .... ●
- .... ●

EXTRAS

- .... ●
- .... ●
- .... ●
- .... ●
- .... ●
- .... ●
- .... ●
- .... ●
- .... ●
- .... ●

.... **COST**

Weekly Meal Planner

Date....................

#WMMEALPLANNING

WHAT NEEDS USING UP?

....
....
....
....
....
....
....

NOTES – EVENTS TO REMEMBER

....
....
....
....
....
....

	BREAKFAST	LUNCH	DINNER	SNACKS AND PUDS
MONDAY				
TUESDAY				
WEDNESDAY				
THURSDAY				
FRIDAY				
SATURDAY				
SUNDAY				

Shopping List

CHILLED

- ....
- ....
- ....
- ....
- ....
- ....
- ....
- ....
- ....
- ....
- ....
- ....
- ....
- ....
- ....
- ....
- ....
- ....
- ....
- ....
- ....
- ....
- ....
- ....

FRUIT & VEG

- ....
- ....
- ....
- ....
- ....
- ....
- ....
- ....
- ....
- ....
- ....
- ....
- ....
- ....
- ....
- ....
- ....
- ....
- ....
- ....
- ....
- ....
- ....
- ....

DATE ....

STORE CUPBOARD

FROZEN

EXTRAS

COST

Embrace the MESS — those full, happy tummies are WORTH it!

Weekly Meal Planner

Date.....................

WHAT NEEDS USING UP?

....
....
....
....
....
....
....

NOTES – EVENTS TO REMEMBER

....
....
....
....
....
....

	BREAKFAST	LUNCH	DINNER	SNACKS AND PUDS
MONDAY				
TUESDAY				
WEDNESDAY				
THURSDAY				
FRIDAY				
SATURDAY				
SUNDAY				

Shopping List

CHILLED

.... ●
.... ●
.... ●
.... ●
.... ●
.... ●
.... ●
.... ●
.... ●
.... ●
.... ●
.... ●
.... ●
.... ●
.... ●
.... ●
.... ●
.... ●
.... ●
.... ●
.... ●
.... ●
.... ●

FRUIT & VEG

.... ●
.... ●
.... ●
.... ●
.... ●
.... ●
.... ●
.... ●
.... ●
.... ●
.... ●
.... ●
.... ●
.... ●
.... ●
.... ●
.... ●
.... ●
.... ●
.... ●
.... ●
.... ●
.... ●

DATE ....

STORE CUPBOARD

FROZEN

EXTRAS

.... COST

Weekly Meal Planner

Date....................

WHAT NEEDS USING UP?

NOTES – EVENTS TO REMEMBER

	BREAKFAST	LUNCH	DINNER	SNACKS AND PUDS
MONDAY				
TUESDAY				
WEDNESDAY				
THURSDAY				
FRIDAY				
SATURDAY				
SUNDAY				

Shopping List

CHILLED

.... ●
.... ●
.... ●
.... ●
.... ●
.... ●
.... ●
.... ●
.... ●
.... ●
.... ●
.... ●
.... ●
.... ●
.... ●
.... ●
.... ●
.... ●
.... ●
.... ●
.... ●
.... ●

FRUIT & VEG

.... ●
.... ●
.... ●
.... ●
.... ●
.... ●
.... ●
.... ●
.... ●
.... ●
.... ●
.... ●
.... ●
.... ●
.... ●
.... ●
.... ●
.... ●
.... ●
.... ●
.... ●
.... ●

DATE ....

STORE CUPBOARD

FROZEN

EXTRAS

COST

Weekly Meal Planner

Date....................

WHAT NEEDS USING UP?

....
....
....
....
....
....
....

NOTES – EVENTS TO REMEMBER

....
....
....
....
....
....

	BREAKFAST	LUNCH	DINNER	SNACKS AND PUDS
MONDAY				
TUESDAY				
WEDNESDAY				
THURSDAY				
FRIDAY				
SATURDAY				
SUNDAY				

Shopping List

CHILLED

....
....
....
....
....
....
....
....
....
....
....
....
....
....
....
....
....
....
....
....
....
....

FRUIT & VEG

....
....
....
....
....
....
....
....
....
....
....
....
....
....
....
....
....
....
....
....
....
....

DATE ....

STORE CUPBOARD

- ....
- ....
- ....
- ....
- ....
- ....
- ....
- ....
- ....
- ....
- ....
- ....
- ....
- ....
- ....
- ....
- ....
- ....
- ....
- ....
- ....
- ....
- ....
- ....
- ....
- ....
- ....

FROZEN

- ....
- ....
- ....
- ....
- ....
- ....
- ....
- ....
- ....
- ....
- ....
- ....
- ....
- ....

EXTRAS

- ....
- ....
- ....
- ....
- ....
- ....
- ....
- ....
- ....
- ....

.... COST

Weekly Meal Planner

Date.....................

WHAT NEEDS USING UP?

....
....
....
....
....
....
....

NOTES – EVENTS TO REMEMBER

....
....
....
....
....
....

	BREAKFAST	LUNCH	DINNER	SNACKS AND PUDS
MONDAY				
TUESDAY				
WEDNESDAY				
THURSDAY				
FRIDAY				
SATURDAY				
SUNDAY				

Shopping List

CHILLED

- ....
- ....
- ....
- ....
- ....
- ....
- ....
- ....
- ....
- ....
- ....
- ....
- ....
- ....
- ....
- ....
- ....
- ....
- ....
- ....
- ....
- ....

FRUIT & VEG

- ....
- ....
- ....
- ....
- ....
- ....
- ....
- ....
- ....
- ....
- ....
- ....
- ....
- ....
- ....
- ....
- ....
- ....
- ....
- ....
- ....
- ....

DATE ....

STORE CUPBOARD

FROZEN

EXTRAS

COST ....

Weekly Meal Planner

Date.....................

WHAT NEEDS USING UP?

....
....
....
....
....
....
....

NOTES – EVENTS TO REMEMBER

....
....
....
....
....
....

	BREAKFAST	LUNCH	DINNER	SNACKS AND PUDS
MONDAY				
TUESDAY				
WEDNESDAY				
THURSDAY				
FRIDAY				
SATURDAY				
SUNDAY				

Shopping List

CHILLED

.... ●
.... ●
.... ●
.... ●
.... ●
.... ●
.... ●
.... ●
.... ●
.... ●
.... ●
.... ●
.... ●
.... ●
.... ●
.... ●
.... ●
.... ●
.... ●
.... ●
.... ●
.... ●
.... ●

FRUIT & VEG

.... ●
.... ●
.... ●
.... ●
.... ●
.... ●
.... ●
.... ●
.... ●
.... ●
.... ●
.... ●
.... ●
.... ●
.... ●
.... ●
.... ●
.... ●
.... ●
.... ●
.... ●
.... ●
.... ●

DATE ....

STORE CUPBOARD

FROZEN

EXTRAS

COST

Weekly Meal Planner

Date..................

WHAT NEEDS USING UP?

NOTES – EVENTS TO REMEMBER

	BREAKFAST	LUNCH	DINNER	SNACKS AND PUDS
MONDAY				
TUESDAY				
WEDNESDAY				
THURSDAY				
FRIDAY				
SATURDAY				
SUNDAY				

Shopping List

CHILLED

....
....
....
....
....
....
....
....
....
....
....
....
....
....
....
....
....
....
....
....
....
....

FRUIT & VEG

....
....
....
....
....
....
....
....
....
....
....
....
....
....
....
....
....
....
....
....
....
....

DATE ....

STORE CUPBOARD

FROZEN

EXTRAS

TAKE FIVE
MINUTES FOR
YOU TODAY,
you deserve
A BREAK!

Weekly Meal Planner

Date....................

WHAT NEEDS USING UP?

NOTES – EVENTS TO REMEMBER

	BREAKFAST	LUNCH	DINNER	SNACKS AND PUDS
MONDAY				
TUESDAY				
WEDNESDAY				
THURSDAY				
FRIDAY				
SATURDAY				
SUNDAY				

Shopping List

CHILLED

- ....
- ....
- ....
- ....
- ....
- ....
- ....
- ....
- ....
- ....
- ....
- ....
- ....
- ....
- ....
- ....
- ....
- ....
- ....
- ....
- ....
- ....

FRUIT & VEG

- ....
- ....
- ....
- ....
- ....
- ....
- ....
- ....
- ....
- ....
- ....
- ....
- ....
- ....
- ....
- ....
- ....
- ....
- ....
- ....
- ....
- ....

DATE ....

STORE CUPBOARD

FROZEN

EXTRAS

Weekly Meal Planner

Date...................

WHAT NEEDS USING UP?

....
....
....
....
....
....
....

NOTES – EVENTS TO REMEMBER

....
....
....
....
....
....

	BREAKFAST	LUNCH	DINNER	SNACKS AND PUDS
MONDAY				
TUESDAY				
WEDNESDAY				
THURSDAY				
FRIDAY				
SATURDAY				
SUNDAY				

Shopping List

CHILLED

- ....
- ....
- ....
- ....
- ....
- ....
- ....
- ....
- ....
- ....
- ....
- ....
- ....
- ....
- ....
- ....
- ....
- ....
- ....
- ....
- ....
- ....

FRUIT & VEG

- ....
- ....
- ....
- ....
- ....
- ....
- ....
- ....
- ....
- ....
- ....
- ....
- ....
- ....
- ....
- ....
- ....
- ....
- ....
- ....
- ....
- ....

DATE ....

STORE CUPBOARD

FROZEN

EXTRAS

Weekly Meal Planner

Date....................

WHAT NEEDS USING UP?

NOTES – EVENTS TO REMEMBER

	BREAKFAST	LUNCH	DINNER	SNACKS AND PUDS
MONDAY				
TUESDAY				
WEDNESDAY				
THURSDAY				
FRIDAY				
SATURDAY				
SUNDAY				

Shopping List

CHILLED

- .... ●
- .... ●
- .... ●
- .... ●
- .... ●
- .... ●
- .... ●
- .... ●
- .... ●
- .... ●
- .... ●
- .... ●
- .... ●
- .... ●
- .... ●
- .... ●
- .... ●
- .... ●
- .... ●
- .... ●
- .... ●
- .... ●
- .... ●

FRUIT & VEG

- .... ●
- .... ●
- .... ●
- .... ●
- .... ●
- .... ●
- .... ●
- .... ●
- .... ●
- .... ●
- .... ●
- .... ●
- .... ●
- .... ●
- .... ●
- .... ●
- .... ●
- .... ●
- .... ●
- .... ●
- .... ●
- .... ●
- .... ●

DATE ....

STORE CUPBOARD

FROZEN

EXTRAS

Weekly Meal Planner

Date...................

WHAT NEEDS USING UP?

....
....
....
....
....
....
....

NOTES – EVENTS TO REMEMBER

....
....
....
....
....
....

	BREAKFAST	LUNCH	DINNER	SNACKS AND PUDS
MONDAY				
TUESDAY				
WEDNESDAY				
THURSDAY				
FRIDAY				
SATURDAY				
SUNDAY				

Shopping List

CHILLED

.... ●
.... ●
.... ●
.... ●
.... ●
.... ●
.... ●
.... ●
.... ●
.... ●
.... ●
.... ●
.... ●
.... ●
.... ●
.... ●
.... ●
.... ●
.... ●
.... ●
.... ●

FRUIT & VEG

.... ●
.... ●
.... ●
.... ●
.... ●
.... ●
.... ●
.... ●
.... ●
.... ●
.... ●
.... ●
.... ●
.... ●
.... ●
.... ●
.... ●
.... ●
.... ●
.... ●
.... ●

DATE ....

STORE CUPBOARD

- ....
- ....
- ....
- ....
- ....
- ....
- ....
- ....
- ....
- ....
- ....
- ....
- ....
- ....
- ....
- ....
- ....
- ....
- ....
- ....
- ....
- ....
- ....
- ....
- ....
- ....

FROZEN

- ....
- ....
- ....
- ....
- ....
- ....
- ....
- ....
- ....
- ....
- ....
- ....
- ....
- ....

EXTRAS

- ....
- ....
- ....
- ....
- ....
- ....
- ....
- ....
- ....
- ....

.... COST

Weekly Meal Planner

Date.....................

WHAT NEEDS USING UP?

....
....
....
....
....
....
....

NOTES – EVENTS TO REMEMBER

....
....
....
....
....
....

	BREAKFAST	LUNCH	DINNER	SNACKS AND PUDS
MONDAY				
TUESDAY				
WEDNESDAY				
THURSDAY				
FRIDAY				
SATURDAY				
SUNDAY				

Shopping List

CHILLED

- ....
- ....
- ....
- ....
- ....
- ....
- ....
- ....
- ....
- ....
- ....
- ....
- ....
- ....
- ....
- ....
- ....
- ....
- ....
- ....
- ....
- ....

FRUIT & VEG

- ....
- ....
- ....
- ....
- ....
- ....
- ....
- ....
- ....
- ....
- ....
- ....
- ....
- ....
- ....
- ....
- ....
- ....
- ....
- ....
- ....
- ....

DATE ....

STORE CUPBOARD

FROZEN

EXTRAS

.... COST

Weekly Meal Planner

Date...................

WHAT NEEDS USING UP?

NOTES – EVENTS TO REMEMBER

	BREAKFAST	LUNCH	DINNER	SNACKS AND PUDS
MONDAY				
TUESDAY				
WEDNESDAY				
THURSDAY				
FRIDAY				
SATURDAY				
SUNDAY				

Shopping List

CHILLED

· ●
· ●
· ●
· ●
· ●
· ●
· ●
· ●
· ●
· ●
· ●
· ●
· ●
· ●
· ●
· ●
· ●
· ●
· ●
· ●

FRUIT & VEG

· ●
· ●
· ●
· ●
· ●
· ●
· ●
· ●
· ●
· ●
· ●
· ●
· ●
· ●
· ●
· ●
· ●
· ●
· ●
· ●

DATE · · · · · · · · · · · · · · · · · ·

STORE CUPBOARD

FROZEN

EXTRAS

.... COST

THE SECRET TO A

STRESS-FREE

TOMORROW,

is a little
planning today

Weekly Meal Planner

Date....................

WHAT NEEDS USING UP?

NOTES – EVENTS TO REMEMBER

	BREAKFAST	LUNCH	DINNER	SNACKS AND PUDS
MONDAY				
TUESDAY				
WEDNESDAY				
THURSDAY				
FRIDAY				
SATURDAY				
SUNDAY				

Shopping List

CHILLED

.... ●
.... ●
.... ●
.... ●
.... ●
.... ●
.... ●
.... ●
.... ●
.... ●
.... ●
.... ●
.... ●
.... ●
.... ●
.... ●
.... ●
.... ●
.... ●
.... ●
.... ●
.... ●
.... ●

FRUIT & VEG

.... ●
.... ●
.... ●
.... ●
.... ●
.... ●
.... ●
.... ●
.... ●
.... ●
.... ●
.... ●
.... ●
.... ●
.... ●
.... ●
.... ●
.... ●
.... ●
.... ●
.... ●
.... ●
.... ●

DATE ....

STORE CUPBOARD

....

....

....

....

....

....

....

....

....

....

....

....

....

....

....

....

....

....

....

....

....

....

....

....

....

FROZEN

....

....

....

....

....

....

....

....

....

....

....

....

....

....

EXTRAS

....

....

....

....

....

....

....

....

....

.... COST

Weekly Meal Planner

Date...................

WHAT NEEDS USING UP?

....
....
....
....
....
....
....

NOTES – EVENTS TO REMEMBER

....
....
....
....
....
....

	BREAKFAST	LUNCH	DINNER	SNACKS AND PUDS
MONDAY				
TUESDAY				
WEDNESDAY				
THURSDAY				
FRIDAY				
SATURDAY				
SUNDAY				

Shopping List

CHILLED

· ●
· ●
· ●
· ●
· ●
· ●
· ●
· ●
· ●
· ●
· ●
· ●
· ●
· ●
· ●
· ●
· ●
· ●
· ●
· ●
· ●

FRUIT & VEG

· ●
· ●
· ●
· ●
· ●
· ●
· ●
· ●
· ●
· ●
· ●
· ●
· ●
· ●
· ●
· ●
· ●
· ●
· ●
· ●
· ●

DATE · · · · · · · · · · · ·

STORE CUPBOARD

....

....

....

....

....

....

....

....

....

....

....

....

....

....

....

....

....

....

....

....

....

....

....

....

FROZEN

....

....

....

....

....

....

....

....

....

....

....

....

....

EXTRAS

....

....

....

....

....

....

....

....

....

.... **COST**

Weekly Meal Planner

Date.....................

WHAT NEEDS USING UP?

NOTES – EVENTS TO REMEMBER

	BREAKFAST	LUNCH	DINNER	SNACKS AND PUDS
MONDAY				
TUESDAY				
WEDNESDAY				
THURSDAY				
FRIDAY				
SATURDAY				
SUNDAY				

Shopping List

CHILLED

.... ●
.... ●
.... ●
.... ●
.... ●
.... ●
.... ●
.... ●
.... ●
.... ●
.... ●
.... ●
.... ●
.... ●
.... ●
.... ●
.... ●
.... ●
.... ●
.... ●

FRUIT & VEG

.... ●
.... ●
.... ●
.... ●
.... ●
.... ●
.... ●
.... ●
.... ●
.... ●
.... ●
.... ●
.... ●
.... ●
.... ●
.... ●
.... ●
.... ●
.... ●
.... ●

DATE ....

STORE CUPBOARD

FROZEN

EXTRAS

COST

Weekly Meal Planner

Date....................

WHAT NEEDS USING UP?

....
....
....
....
....
....
....

NOTES – EVENTS TO REMEMBER

....
....
....
....
....

	BREAKFAST	LUNCH	DINNER	SNACKS AND PUDS
MONDAY				
TUESDAY				
WEDNESDAY				
THURSDAY				
FRIDAY				
SATURDAY				
SUNDAY				

Shopping List

CHILLED

- ....
- ....
- ....
- ....
- ....
- ....
- ....
- ....
- ....
- ....
- ....
- ....
- ....
- ....
- ....
- ....
- ....
- ....
- ....
- ....
- ....
- ....
- ....

FRUIT & VEG

- ....
- ....
- ....
- ....
- ....
- ....
- ....
- ....
- ....
- ....
- ....
- ....
- ....
- ....
- ....
- ....
- ....
- ....
- ....
- ....
- ....
- ....
- ....

DATE ....

STORE CUPBOARD

FROZEN

EXTRAS

COST

Weekly Meal Planner

Date.....................

WHAT NEEDS USING UP?

NOTES – EVENTS TO REMEMBER

	BREAKFAST	LUNCH	DINNER	SNACKS AND PUDS
MONDAY				
TUESDAY				
WEDNESDAY				
THURSDAY				
FRIDAY				
SATURDAY				
SUNDAY				

Shopping List

CHILLED

.... ●
.... ●
.... ●
.... ●
.... ●
.... ●
.... ●
.... ●
.... ●
.... ●
.... ●
.... ●
.... ●
.... ●
.... ●
.... ●
.... ●
.... ●
.... ●
.... ●
.... ●
.... ●

FRUIT & VEG

.... ●
.... ●
.... ●
.... ●
.... ●
.... ●
.... ●
.... ●
.... ●
.... ●
.... ●
.... ●
.... ●
.... ●
.... ●
.... ●
.... ●
.... ●
.... ●
.... ●
.... ●
.... ●

DATE ....

STORE CUPBOARD

FROZEN

EXTRAS

COST ....

Weekly Meal Planner

Date....................

WHAT NEEDS USING UP?

....
....
....
....
....
....

NOTES – EVENTS TO REMEMBER

....
....
....
....
....

	BREAKFAST	LUNCH	DINNER	SNACKS AND PUDS
MONDAY				
TUESDAY				
WEDNESDAY				
THURSDAY				
FRIDAY				
SATURDAY				
SUNDAY				

Shopping List

CHILLED

FRUIT & VEG

DATE ....

STORE CUPBOARD

FROZEN

EXTRAS

COST

THERE'S NO
SUCH THING
AS THE

perfect

parent.

SO JUST DO YOU!

Weekly Meal Planner

Date......................

WHAT NEEDS USING UP?

....
....
....
....
....
....
....

NOTES – EVENTS TO REMEMBER

....
....
....
....
....
....

	BREAKFAST	LUNCH	DINNER	SNACKS AND PUDS
MONDAY				
TUESDAY				
WEDNESDAY				
THURSDAY				
FRIDAY				
SATURDAY				
SUNDAY				

Shopping List

CHILLED

.... •
.... •
.... •
.... •
.... •
.... •
.... •
.... •
.... •
.... •
.... •
.... •
.... •
.... •
.... •
.... •
.... •
.... •
.... •
.... •
.... •
.... •

FRUIT & VEG

.... •
.... •
.... •
.... •
.... •
.... •
.... •
.... •
.... •
.... •
.... •
.... •
.... •
.... •
.... •
.... •
.... •
.... •
.... •
.... •
.... •
.... •

DATE ....

STORE CUPBOARD

FROZEN

EXTRAS

.... COST

Weekly Meal Planner

Date....................

WHAT NEEDS USING UP?

NOTES – EVENTS TO REMEMBER

	BREAKFAST	LUNCH	DINNER	SNACKS AND PUDS
MONDAY				
TUESDAY				
WEDNESDAY				
THURSDAY				
FRIDAY				
SATURDAY				
SUNDAY				

Penguin
Random
House

Photographer Clare Winfield
Food stylist Maud Eden
Prop stylist Wei Tang
Nutritionist Lucy Upton
Editor Rebecca Woods
Designer Georgie Hewitt
Jacket Designer Amy Cox
Jacket Coordinator Lucy Philpott
Senior Production Editor Tony Phipps
Senior Production Controller Stephanie McConnell
Managing Art Editor Bess Daly
Senior Acquisitions Editor Stephanie Milner
Art Director Maxine Pedliham
Publishing Director Katie Cowan

First published in Great Britain in 2020 by
Dorling Kindersley Limited
One Embassy Gardens, 8 Viaduct Gardens,
London, SW11 7BW

Text copyright © 2020 Rebecca Wilson
Copyright © 2020 Dorling Kindersley Limited
A Penguin Random House Company
10 9 8 7 6 5 4 3 2 1
001–324126–Dec/2020

A CIP catalogue record for this book
is available from the British Library.
ISBN: 978-0-2415-0754-4
Printed and bound in China

For the curious

www.dk.com

PLEASE NOTE

• All eggs are medium (UK) or large
(US) unless otherwise specified.
Uncooked or partially cooked eggs
should not be served to those with
compromised immune systems.
• Those following strict allergen diets
should always check the packet for
guidance about suitability.
• Soy sauce is normally very high in
salt and not recommended for use in
baby or toddlers foods for this reason.
Choosing a lower salt soy sauce can be
therefore be a good swap for the
whole family – but be careful each
brand is different with some still
containing too much salt. Try to chose
a low salt variety that has less than
6g/100mls of salt on the label

STILL HUNGRY?
Follow @whatmummymakes
for much more.

MIX
Paper from
responsible sources
FSC™ C018179

This book was made with Forest Stewardship
Council ™ certified paper – one small step in
DK's commitment to a sustainable future.
For more information go to
www.dk.com/our-green-pledge